ENGLISH SEVEN TO TWELVE

3

D. Hughes and A. Josephs

Illustrated by T. Wanless

CollinsEducational

© 1979 D. Hughes & A. Josephs
0 00 314319 8
First impression 1979
This impression 1993
Printed in Hong Kong

Notes for teachers

This book is the third of a series of five, the aim of which is to provide teachers of the 7–12 age group with a structured scheme for the teaching of a wide range of basic English skills. One of the main features is the use, as stimulus material, of extracts from recent children's fiction of acknowledged high quality.

The book follows the same pattern as the first two books in the series. It has thirty Units, each of which fits into an overall pattern, whilst having a distinct unity of its own, based on six sections closely linked to the initial stimulus. Many of the sections offer two types of related tasks. The presentation is practical and each Unit is completely contained within a four-page spread. An additional feature of Book 3 is the inclusion, from Unit 4 onwards, of reference skill work linked to both the picture and the passage.

Unit pattern

1 The opening passage (mainly prose but sometimes verse) is the key to the whole Unit and each of the other sections is closely linked to it. A major aim is to excite interest in the books from which the passages are taken, and the book list on page 126 will act as a valuable class library list.

2 The comprehension questions ('Understanding'), as well as testing thorough and accurate reading and summary skills, also present opportunities for individual thought and opinion. One particular intention has been to allow the less able child the chance to offer answers which are acceptable if not as elaborate as those provided by the more able.

3 'My own work' uses the opening passage as the stimulus for creative writing. Again the aim has been for every child to be motivated to find a successful response.

4 The picture is intended primarily to act as the stimulus for a creative response as well as for oral activities. The link between the picture and the passage is deliberately a loose one, to encourage a wide range of response from both teacher and child.

5 From Unit 4 onwards work concerning reference skills is provided, linked to both the picture and the passage, but **not** intended to prevent the creative and discursive use of the picture. The work should prove interesting and valuable in promoting the development of such skills as listing, classifying, labelling, making headings and notes, thus providing practice in the organisational skills needed in topic and project work. Questions on the use of dictionaries, encyclopaedias and other works of reference are included, with the assumption that the children will have access to good examples of such books.

6 This section is a constant factor, in testing the basic skills of handwriting, vocabulary, sentence structure, punctuation, spelling etc.

7 The last section ('Language') introduces new language skills or reinforces others already introduced. Technical terms are gradually made known in this book and a key to the skills being tested is included in the list of contents. In this section, as in sections 2, 5 and 6, a systematic approach is followed, based for the most part around patterns of five or ten questions. Such a pattern will aid both sentence and composition structure.

Contents

Reference skill	Principal language skill
	Capital letters
	Participles
	Paragraph structure
Classifying and defining	Nouns and verbs
Classifying and listing	Adjectives and adverbs
Directory list and alphabetical order	Pronouns and conjunctions
Classifying and listing details	Adverbial phrases
Observing, classifying and listing details	Proper nouns
Use of dictionary and specialist word-list	Collective nouns
Labelling	Relative pronouns
Technical terms and labelling	Future tense
Dictionary definitions	Inverted commas
Use of encyclopaedia and summarising	Adverbial phrases
Observing and listing in order of importance	Participles
Encyclopaedia work and note-making	Prefixes
Headings and relevant lists	Quotation marks
Information from timetables	Comparative of adjectives
Use of dictionary – word order	Prepositions
Notice making – relevant information	Past/passed etc.
Use of dictionary – accurate word selection	This, that, these, those
Listing relevant information	Relative pronouns
Notice making – relevant detail	Ought, should, must
Details from pictorial information	Synonyms
Compiling specialist word-list in dictionary form	Apostrophes
Close observation of pictorial detail	Suffixes
Encyclopaedia work and note-making	Commas
Compiling specialist word-list	Synonyms and antonyms
Atlas work and use of specialist index	Similes
Plan-making and labelling	Revision
Project work and book design	Revision

First steps in writing

Ramona wished she had a *K* in her name, so that she could give it a nice straight back. Ramona enjoyed Miss Binney's descriptions of the letters of the alphabet and listened for them while she worked. In front of her Susan played with a curl while she worked. She twisted it around her finger, stretched it out, and let it go. *Boing*, thought Ramona automatically.

"Ramona, let's keep our eyes on our work," said Miss Binney. "No, Davy. *D* faces the *other* way."

Once more Ramona bent over her paper. The hardest part of her name, she soon discovered, was getting the right number of points on the *M* and *N*. Sometimes her name came out RANOMA. But before long she remembered that two points came first. "Good work, Ramona," said Miss Binney, the first time Ramona printed her name correctly. Ramona hugged herself with happiness and love for Miss Binney. Soon, she was sure, she would be able to join her letters together and write her name in the same rumply grown-up way that Beezus wrote her name.

Then Ramona discovered that some boys and girls had an extra letter followed by a dot. "Miss Binney, why don't I have a letter with a dot after it?" she asked.

"Because we have only one Ramona," said Miss Binney. "We have two Erics. Eric Jones and Eric Ryan. We call them Eric J. and Eric R., because we don't want to get our Erics mixed up."

Ramona did not like to miss anything. "Could I have another letter with a little dot?" she asked, knowing that Miss Binney would not think she was pestering.

Miss Binney smiled and leaned over Ramona's table. "Of course you may. This is the way to make a *Q*. A nice round *O* with a little tail like a cat. And there is your little dot, which is called a full stop." Then Miss Binney walked on, supervising seat work.

Ramona was charmed by her last initial. She drew a nice round *O* beside the one Miss Binney had drawn, and then she added a tail before she leaned back to admire her work. She had one balloon and two Hallowe'en hats in her first name and a cat in her last name. She doubted if anyone else in the morning kindergarten had such an interesting name.

from 'Ramona the Pest' by Beverly Cleary

Understanding

1　What work were the children doing?

2　Why did Ramona wish she had a *K* in her name?

3　What was Ramona listening for while she worked?

4　What was Susan doing that attracted Ramona's attention?

5　Why did Ramona sometimes write her name as RANOMA?

6　Why was Ramona so happy when she wrote her name correctly?

7　Why did Ramona ask Miss Binney for another letter with a dot?

8　Why did Miss Binney give her a *Q*?

9　What were the two Hallowe'en hats and the balloon in Ramona's name?

10　What method did Miss Binney use to help the children remember the letters?

My own work

Describe some of the things you remember doing in your first year at school.

Handwriting

A   Here are ten popular children's names of today. Write them out in alphabetical order, in your best handwriting.

     Peter   Susan   Andrew   Nicola   David
     Elizabeth   Mark   Alison   Paul   Julie

B   Now make a list of ten other names you know. Put this list in alphabetical order as well.

Language

In the passage Miss Binney helped the children to remember the shapes of the capital letters. She did this by comparing them with interesting objects. For example, she said a *Q* was an *O* with a little tail like a cat.

How do you think Miss Binney would have helped the children to remember the shapes of these capital letters?

O T H X S B D F U Z

Write a sentence about each one. The first one is done for you.

1   The letter **O** is shaped like a balloon.

Getting Back

Coming back to school again –
All our crowd together –
What a lot of ways we've been
In many kinds of weather!
After all our journeyings,
We see familiar faces
And show each other all the things
We've brought from different places.

Jack has thrilling tales he tells
Of trails and mountain-reaches;
Constance has a box of shells
And agates from the beaches;
Mary saw the Capitol
From corner stone to dome;
And Jim has camera shots of all
His summer hikes at home.

Talking, laughing, looking out
To greet the latest comer –
We may finish, but we doubt
Our getting through, till summer!
We must hear it all – we must
See each stone and feather –
And the best of all is just
Getting back together!

Dorothy Brown Thompson

Understanding

1   What time of year do you think the poem is describing?

2   Why are the children so excited at seeing each other again?

3   Write a sentence about **each** of the four children mentioned in the second verse, saying what each has been doing.

4   Why does the poet think the children will not finish talking till summer?

5   What does the poet say she likes best of all?

My own work

Write a story about the best holiday or the best day out you have ever had.

Spelling

In the first verse of the poem you will see the word <u>we've</u> used as a short way of writing <u>we have</u>. This is called an **abbreviation**.

What is each of the following an abbreviation of?

you've	I'm	wasn't	don't	can't
she's	I'll	didn't	they're	who's

Language

In the third verse of the poem the children are described as <u>talking</u>, <u>laughing</u>, <u>looking out</u>.

Write down ten more words ending in <u>ing</u> that describe things that children like to do.

unit 3

The wonderful marrow

On the Friday evening Mr. Morgan and David, under a big black umbrella, took a last look at the marrow. It looked wonderful. It was striped pale green and dark green, like a football jersey. It swelled in the middle and tapered elegantly at each end. While they were admiring it Mr. Hughes, two gardens away, came out with a knife. He cut his marrow and gathered it up, plastic tent and all, and carried it indoors.

David went to bed. His room smelled funny, because of the damp patch. The rain on the roof soothed him. He fell asleep. In the middle of the night he woke up, thinking he had heard thunder. He fell asleep again, then woke again. He couldn't understand the silence. Then he realized the rain had stopped. The light outside his window was the moon. He fell asleep, watching the raindrops sparkle on the window panes.

He woke up early. The sun was shining and the birds were twittering. Through his window he could see the blue mountain. It was the first time he had seen it for five days. He jumped out of bed and put on his grey shorts, his striped shirt and his gym shoes. He went downstairs and ate four ginger biscuits, to make him last until breakfast. He went out into his Dad's shed to get the wheelbarrow. Mr. Morgan hadn't got a wheelbarrow so David's Dad was lending him his to lug the marrow to the church hall in.

He wheeled the wheelbarrow round to Mr. Morgan's garden to have it ready. He thought, "I'll take the old box off the marrow. Give it a bit of sun, like."

He left the wheelbarrow by Mr. Morgan's back door. He began to walk down the jam-jar-cobbled path. He stopped. He could not believe what he saw. Where once the bottom of Mr. Morgan's garden had been was an enormous gaping hole!

It was a huge hole, as wide as the garden and yards across. On each side a length of fence – Mr. Evans's and David's – leaned over the hole, as if about to topple in. The beans were gone, the cabbages and tomatoes were gone. Half the broken dinner plates and jam-jar bottoms were gone. Worst of all, the entire marrow bed was gone, complete with Mr. Morgan's marrow.

from 'Mr. Morgan's Marrow' by Prudence Andrew

Understanding

1 What is a marrow?

2 What does the passage tell you about the shape of Mr. Morgan's marrow?

3 What does the passage tell you about its colour?

4 What does the passage tell you about its size?

5 Where was the marrow growing?

6 How do you know it had been raining heavily?

7 David woke twice during the night. What made him wake up on **each** occasion?

8 Why do you think he woke up early in the morning?

9 Why could he now see the blue mountains?

10 Why do you think David needed his Dad's wheelbarrow?

My own work

Something strange had happened while David was in bed. Write a story describing what happened during the night.

Words

Near the end of the first paragraph is the word <u>plastic</u>. A number of words end with the two letters <u>ic</u>. Here is a list of five more.

picnic   magic   comic   music   fantastic

Write five sentences about **yourself**. In each sentence use **one** of the words from the list.

Language

Below are written out the five sentences of the paragraph that is next to the last one in the passage. The sentences are in the **wrong** order.

Without looking back at the passage write out the sentences in the **right** order. When you have done so, check to see if you are right.

He stopped.
He began to walk down the jam-jar-cobbled path.
Where once the bottom of Mr. Morgan's garden had been was an
    enormous gaping hole!
He could not believe what he saw.
He left the wheelbarrow by Mr. Morgan's back door.

17

Looking after the shop

On Monday mornings Mr. Toddy went to wind all the clocks up at the Big House. He had been doing it for years and years. Sometimes he allowed Pipsy to go with him in her school holidays.

This Monday Mr. Toddy had asked Pipsy if she would like to stay and look after the shop instead of going with him.

When she arrived, Mr. Toddy was ready to go. His bowler hat was pressed down over his ears and he clutched his shabby umbrella, although the sun was shining. In the other hand he had a little leather case in which he carried clock oil, keys, and tools he might need up at the Big House. He was peering over his half-moon spectacles at her.

"I'll leave Old Prince with you today," he said. "Now, keep the bottom half of the door locked, and tell anyone who comes that I shall be back in an hour." Pipsy watched him shuffle off round the corner.

She had the shop all to herself!

"Good Old Prince, isn't this fun!" she cried. "What can we do to give Mr. Toddy a surprise when he gets back?"

First she fed the canary, because that was a job she did every day. Then she wandered round the shop, pretending everything in it was hers. She practised fixing the black eye-glass into her eye, and trying to keep it there without holding on to it.

Then she stood and looked up at the giant skittle clock. Did it strike four times, one for each clock face? she wondered. Suppose she were to wind it to find out? Mr. Toddy kept a box of clock keys behind the counter.

The keys were in a muddle. She took one out and read the label. Mr. Toddy's spiky old-fashioned writing was difficult to under- stand, but she read: TOMPION BRACKET. She knew what that was. As she had found the key, she decided to wind that one first.

She climbed up on to the rickety chair and opened the glass door of the clock face. She wound the clock carefully and set the hands by her own pocket watch.

from 'The Canary Shop' by Rosemary Garland

● Understanding

A 1 What sort of shop did Mr. Toddy own?
    2 How often did Pipsy help Mr. Toddy?
    3 Who else lived in the shop with Mr. Toddy?
    4 How do you know Pipsy enjoyed looking after the shop for Mr. Toddy?
    5 What do you think the words TOMPION BRACKET were used for?

B What does each of the following tell you about Mr. Toddy?

    1 the way he let Pipsy look after the shop
    2 the fact that he had been going up to the Big House for years and years
    3 his umbrella (when the sun was shining)
    4 his half-moon spectacles
    5 the instructions he gave Pipsy

● My own work

Imagine you have been asked to help in a shop you know well. Write a story about the day you helped in the shop.

The clocks described in the passage gave **information** about the time. The picture shows a pilot's cabin in an aeroplane. The dials give the pilot **information** about such things as speed, height and fuel.

Here are the names of five objects that give information. Make a list of the objects and opposite each one write down the information it gives.

atlas   calendar   dictionary   signpost   thermometer

Spelling

A   Look at the word <u>surprise</u> half-way down the passage. It is a word we have to learn to spell carefully. Complete each of the following sentences. In each case the missing word is in the passage and needs careful spelling.

1 The _____ on the key read TOMPION BRACKET.
2 The sun was _____ but Mr. Toddy still took his umbrella.
3 Pipsy _____ on to the old chair.
4 She wound the clock _____ as she did not want to damage it.
5 Because he used an old pen, Mr. Toddy's _____ was hard to read.

B   Now here are five more sentences to complete. The missing words need careful spelling but this time they are **not** in the passage.

1 Pipsy's mother and _____ bought her a watch for her birthday.
2 On the back of the watch were Pipsy's name and _____.
3 Pipsy borrowed a book on clocks and watches from the school _____.
4 Pipsy's watch showed hours, _____ and seconds.
5 She soon learned that it _____ if she forgot to wind it up.

Language

A   Look at the passage again and write down five naming words (**nouns**) that name things found in Mr. Toddy's shop.

B   Now write a sentence about each of these objects and underline the action words (**verbs**) that you use in each sentence.

unit 5

The missing rabbit

Shadrach was gone! The hutch was empty! Shadrach wasn't in his hutch. Davie stood there in his horrible scare, the forgotten bun squeezing to pieces in his hand. He stared at dim corners of the dark cluttered barn. There was nothing. Nothing moved. The whole barn felt empty. It was frighteningly quiet. He peered at the hutch in the dimness, poked at it, his face close. There was nothing. The cover of the hutch wasn't open – the brick was still on it. There wasn't any hole, not a single one of the slats was loose, nothing was disturbed, but Shadrach was gone.

He crouched at the hutch, frightened and forlorn. In the total Sunday silence of the barn and the village it seemed as if he could hear his own heart thump. He stared at the cluttered dim corners again, but there were so many nooks and holes, he didn't know where to look. He felt utterly helpless, and inside he began crying, but he did not cry out loud. The quiet was too awful to cry in. Now across the village the bell on the church tower started its solemn deep Sunday tones. Faintly far away the bell of the village of Nes began answering it. The two bells talked solemnly back and forth. It was church time.

The two bells went on ringing; there wasn't another sound. There hadn't been any sound in the barn, not a sound, but all of a sudden – there was Shadrach! There he came slowly hopping across the empty middle of the barn. Straight toward the hutch. Davie did not dare move for fear of scaring Shadrach. He crouched there, squeezing the bun. Shadrach came right to him; he even stood up against his knee like a squirrel. Why, Shadrach wanted to sniff the bun! Then he had the little rabbit, he pulled him up in his arms, he hugged him. "Oh, Shadrach, you came. You came. You came," he said brokenly. "Aw, did you want the bun?" He held the bun to Shadrach's mouth, and Shadrach started nibbling it. Shadrach liked buns!

from 'Shadrach' by Meindert De Jong

22

Understanding

1. Where was Shadrach's hutch?
2. What did Davie see when he looked closely at the hutch?
3. Why do you think Davie had come to visit Shadrach?
4. Why do you think he was frightened when he found Shadrach had gone?
5. Why did it seem he could hear his heart thumping?
6. Why did he cry inside and not aloud?
7. What disturbed the silence of the barn?
8. Why did Davie keep very still when he saw Shadrach?
9. What do you think proved to Davie that Shadrach was all right?
10. What do you think Davie felt when he held Shadrach in his arms?

My own work

The passage describes a very **quiet** place. Some places are very **noisy**. Write about a place you know that is noisy. If you wish you may write about more than one place.

The passage and the picture include animals that are kept as **pets**. Other animals are **wild**, while some are kept for **work**.

Make three lists with the headings **Pets**, **Wild animals** and **Work animals**. Under each heading write the names of five suitable animals.

Sentences

In the passage you will find a number of very short sentences, like, 'Nothing moved.' in the first paragraph. Short sentences often help to make a story more exciting.

Write another paragraph to add to the end of the passage. In this paragraph imagine that Davie heard footsteps outside the barn.

Remember to use a short sentence when the story becomes exciting.

Language

A At the beginning of the second paragraph of the passage two good describing words (**adjectives**) are used to describe Davie when he found Shadrach was missing. These words are <u>frightened</u> and <u>forlorn.</u>

Write down five adjectives that could have been used to describe David when he realised Shadrach was safe.

B At the end of the second paragraph the word <u>solemnly</u> is used to describe **how** the bells were talking. Words that tell you more about verbs in this way are called **adverbs**.

Complete each of the following sentences with a good adverb.

1 Davie was whistling _____ when he opened the door of the barn.
2 When he saw Shadrach had gone, Davie searched _____.
3 His heart beat _____.
4 Suddenly Shadrach hopped _____ across the barn.
5 That night Davie thought _____ about what had happened.

Nobody to play with

Little O was alone at home. She had had measles. But the rash had gone and she was already up again, although she couldn't go out just yet. The Urchin and Knut were to have kept her company, because Mummy had gone out to a sewing circle. But Pelle Göran from number thirty-nine had come along and asked if the Urchin would go and play in his garden. And the Urchin had gone. Then Knut had had to go to the library with a book. And of course he got stuck there. And as a result Little O was quite alone.

At first she played with her dolls for a bit. Then she drew little men and looked at picture books. But she had been doing that for a whole week so it soon became boring.

Then she went out into the hall and put up all the umbrellas and tried to pretend she was living in a tent. But living alone in a tent isn't any fun either. You need at least two people for that, she thought. Fancy none of the others coming home! She thought there must be a thousand games they would be able to play together, but not a single one that could be played all alone.

Then she caught sight of the telephone on the hall table. It would be rather fun to ring up somebody and chat for a bit. She wouldn't feel so forsaken, then. But did she dare?

She had often talked to Daddy and Aunt Bella over the phone. But someone else had always rung up for her. She mustn't ring up all by herself, for she was too little said the others. She couldn't read numbers yet. Well, she could count up to twenty, but she didn't understand the numbers on the dial. If she tried to ring up sometimes, either Mummy or somebody else would always come and take the receiver away from her.

"Ring up on your own telephone," they said.

That stupid old red toy telephone that couldn't answer a word!

But now that none of the others were at home they couldn't prevent her from ringing up on the real one. That decided the matter.

Little O clambered up on to a chair and lifted the receiver.

from 'Little O' by Edith Unnerstad

Understanding

1 Why couldn't Little O go out?
2 Why was she alone in the house?
3 Why did she become bored so quickly?
4 Why did she stop playing at tents?
5 Why did she feel happier when she saw the telephone?
6 Why had she never been allowed to use the telephone on her own?
7 What happened if she did try to use it?
8 Why did her own toy telephone annoy her so much?
9 What finally made her decide to use the real telephone?
10 What does the last sentence tell you about Little O?

My own work

Think back to when you had measles or any other childhood illness. Describe what happened when you were ill and also when you started to get better.

The passage and the picture show how people use the telephone to send messages.

To use a telephone we need a telephone directory that gives details of people's names, addresses and telephone numbers. Here is an example.

Parker John, 11 Cosway St., Newtown	**Newtown** 92216
Parkway Tyre Company, Strand Buildings	**Newtown** 76219
Partington W. E., 20 Coach Rd., Gledhill	**Gledhill** 80236

Write the names of ten members of your class in alphabetical order, as if for a telephone directory. Next to each person's name write down his or her address and telephone number. Make one up for those who have not got a telephone.

● Sentences

Much of the passage is about a telephone. Write a sentence that describes what a telephone is used for.

Now write a sentence about each of the following useful objects found in the home.

television
alarm clock
refrigerator
vacuum cleaner
toaster

● Language

A   In the passage Little O's name is used only **three** times. The word <u>she</u> is used many times to refer to her. Words like <u>she</u> are called **pronouns**.

Write down five more pronouns that you know.

B   The words <u>and</u> and <u>but</u> are also used in the passage. These joining words are called **conjunctions.**

Here are some more conjunctions: <u>because, if, although, until.</u> There are many more conjunctions as well as the six underlined above.

Complete each of the following sentences with a suitable conjunction.

1   Little O was lonely _____ everyone else had gone out.
2   She picked up the telephone _____ she had been told not to do so.
3   At last someone spoke _____ asked her what she wanted.
4   The operator was angry at first _____ laughed when he realised Little O was so young.
5   Her mother told her she could not use the telephone _____ she was old enough to understand the numbers.

The lost bus

Adam began to kick at the creeper. He pushed at it with his foot. Under the leaves some glass appeared.

"Hey!" said Adam. "There's a window here under this plant."

David stared. This time he did come up beside Adam, looking interested at last. They pulled at the creeper with their hands and more glass showed under it. It really was a window – a window that had been hidden away behind the green leaves. It was very dirty, but when they pressed their noses against it and stared through they could see a steering wheel and a driver's seat. Behind that were more seats.

"Do you know what?" David cried. "This is a bus – a truly bus all covered over by the creeper. This is the front window – the windscreen. Here, by my hand, is a windscreen wiper. We are standing on its bonnet. Let's pull the creeper off it."

"We must ask Mr. John Miller," said Adam.

At that moment Mr. John Miller himself appeared, carrying a tray with plates on it. There were scones and little cakes, and mugs of ginger-beer as well.

"Mr. John Miller," Adam called, "we have found a bus in your dump. How did it get here?"

"Well, think of that!" said Mr. John Miller. "I had forgotten it. I bought it years ago and put its engine and wheels on to another bus. The creeper has covered it, but you can pull it off if you like."

Adam saw David's turned-down mouth suddenly turn up at the corners and he smiled all over his face. Adam had never seen such a wide smile. He forgot he was angry with David.

"We can pull the creeper off and make a fort," David cried. "We'll have good fun. We'll eat the cakes first though."

After they had eaten the scones and little cakes, and drunk every drop of ginger-beer, David and Adam began to pull the creeper off the old bus.

It was hard work for there was a lot of creeper and sometimes it was very thick. As they pulled it off, the bus began to show – first the windscreen and bonnet, and then a long row of windows along one side. The windows looked like worried little square eyes peering out from under untidy green hair. The bus was not as tall as most buses because its wheels were gone.

from 'The Bus Under the Leaves' by Margaret Mahy

● Understanding

1 What type of plant is a creeper?
2 How did the boys find the bus?
3 How did they know it was a **bus** they had found?
4 Why had the bus been left in the dump?
5 What condition was the bus in?
6 What effect did finding the bus seem to have on David?
7 How do you know Adam and David had not been too friendly (up to then)?
8 Why do you think the boys were so keen to dig out the bus?
9 Who do you think Mr. John Miller was?
10 Why do you think he had forgotten about the bus?

● My own work

A   Imagine **you** found the bus under the creeper. Describe what you would use it for.

B   Now tell a story about a morning's adventure in the bus with your friends.

The picture shows a place where old cars are broken up, perhaps like the place Mr. John Miller kept. Most of these cars were probably sold more than once. Each time details of the car would have been included in an advertisement.

Here are the names of five cars: Cortina, Mini, Rover, Jaguar, Rolls Royce. Imagine each one is for sale. Make a list of them and make up details under these headings.

type of car	registration number	year of manufacture	colour	price

Words

Look at the next-to-last sentence of the passage. The windows of the bus are described in an interesting way. Now answer these questions about the words the author has used.

1 Why do you think she compared the windows to <u>eyes peering out?</u>
2 Why were the eyes <u>square?</u>
3 Why do you think she thought of the eyes as <u>worried?</u>
4 What was the <u>green hair?</u>
5 Why was it <u>untidy?</u>

Language

Look at the third sentence of the passage. A short **phrase** like <u>Under the leaves</u> is a good way to begin a sentence.

Here are ten more phrases. For each one, complete a sentence about **yourself**.

1 In my bedroom ....
2 For my breakfast ....
3 Near my house ....
4 On the way to school ....
5 In my classroom ....
6 On the wall of the classroom ....
7 Through the window ....
8 At break-time ....
9 In the playground ....
10 After school ....

Names for Twins

Each pair of twins,
rabbits or dogs,
children or frogs,
has to have names
that are almost the same
(to show that they're twins)
but are different too;
so here's what you do.

Find double words,
like Higgledy-Piggledy
(good names for pigs)
or Shilly and Shally
or Dilly and Dally
or Knick and Knack.

Namby and Pamby
are better for poodles;
Whing-Ding for swallows;
Misty and Moisty
and Wishy and Washy
especially for fish.
Call twin kittens
Inky and Pinky
or Helter and Skelter,
or Pell and Mell.
(It's easy to tell
they are twins if their names
have a humdrum sound.)

Crinkum and Crankum
are perfect for squirrels,
like Hanky and Panky
or Fiddle and Faddle;
but Mumbo and Jumbo
are mainly for elephants.
(Airy and Fairy
would never suit *them*.)
Willy and Nilly
will fit almost any twins.
Hubble and Bubble
or Hodge and Podge
or Roly and Poly
are mainly for fat twins.

Chitter and Chatter
or Jingle and Jangle
or Pitter and Patter,
of course, are for noisy twins.
Further than that,
there's Harum and Scarum,
or Hocus and Pocus,
or Heebie and Jeebie,
but these are peculiar,
and have to be used,
like Mixty and Maxty,
for very *odd* pairs . . .
You see what begins
when you have to name twins.

Alastair Reed

Understanding

1 What sort of names does the poet say you should choose for twins?
2 What do you notice about **all** the pairs of names mentioned in the poem?
3 What names does the poet say will fit almost any twins?
4 Why do you think he says Airy and Fairy are unsuitable for elephants?
5 Choose **five** more pairs of names from the poem. In **each** case say why you think the names are suitable **or** unsuitable for twins.

My own work

Choose a pair of names for twins **not** included in the poem. Now write a story about the twins, (which may be children or animals.)

The poem described identical twins. Sometimes twins are almost as alike as the reflection shown in the picture. Most people are **not** alike and one way of describing a person's appearance is to list details about them.

Make a list of ten members of your class and write down their details under these headings.

name	height	weight	colour of hair	colour of eyes	size of shoes

Handwriting

Look again at the names of the twins in the poem. Choose **ten** pairs that seem to you to have an interesting **sound** when you say them. Write out the ten pairs in your best handwriting in the order you like them best.

Language

All the names you have written down in this unit begin with a **capital letter**, because they are **proper nouns**. As well as the names of people, the days of the week, the months of the year and the names of places are proper nouns.

Here is a story to complete. Write out the story, putting a suitable **noun** in each of the gaps. Some of the nouns should be **proper nouns**.

This _____ is about two twins, _____ and _____, who lived in _____.It was the twins' birthday, 22nd _____, and one of their _____ was a game called _____. As it was a cold _____, they were staying indoors to play their new _____. Suddenly there was a _____ at the door. _____ went to answer it. It was their friend _____, who lived in _____ _____, the next road to theirs.

"Look what I've brought for your _____," he shouted.

Then he went quiet as he saw what they were playing. Sadly he gave the _____ a _____, wrapped in coloured _____. They opened the _____ and found another game of _____.

"Never mind," said _____. "We are going to the toy shop on _____ of next week, and we'll change it for another game we like, called _____."

The reindeer in the night

There was a kind of magic about the reindeer slippers, but they were not by any means the first magic things Alan had possessed. He had a knack of finding such treasures. When he was very young there had been a mysterious bluish pebble which, at least in his own opinion, could make him invisible. Later, a couple of swan's feathers had had extraordinary powers – he could all but fly down the stairs when he was holding them. Then there was a wonderful double conker that everybody at school tried to get hold of, for such a thing had never been seen – but that was so strongly magic that it made him unchallenged king of conkers all through the autumn term.

None of these things had been as good as the reindeer slippers.

Alan had been in the middle of measles when they came. When, hot and aching, he woke in the night, he put out his hand to touch the slippers of reindeer hide and he thought that a whole reindeer was there beside him. He felt the hard bones of the beast, like a strong framework over which the beautiful skin was fitted. Then he seemed to be riding on the reindeer's back, hanging on hard to the strong thick neck, sheltering behind the great antlers as he was carried many miles over snowy wastes beneath a huge sky sharp with stars. "What is your name?" he had asked the reindeer. "My name is Swiftly," the creature had replied.

In the morning there were only the reindeer slippers, but night after night Alan and Swiftly rode through deep forests together and across wide plains. As they went, Swiftly would tell Alan of life in the Arctic, of the herds moving darkly over the winter land, of battles when the clash of antlers rang for miles in the ice-bound distances; of the soft-eyed does and their fawns, stepping so lightly that their hoofs barely marked the ground. It was all exactly as described in the book Uncle Stephen had given Alan at the same time as the slippers.

from 'The Reindeer Slippers' by Barbara Willard

Understanding

A Describe the three things that Alan had had when he was younger, which he thought were magic.

B **1** What do you think happened when Alan touched the reindeer slippers during the night?

2 What do you think he remembered best about his ride on the reindeer's back?

3 Why do you think there were only the reindeer slippers in the morning?

4 Which of the stories Swiftly told him do you think Alan would remember best?

5 Why do you think the adventures Swiftly told Alan were just like those in Uncle Stephen's book?

My own work

Choose an object that you own now (or had when you were younger) and which you think of as one of **your** treasures. Describe what it looks like, how you got it and what you've done with it since you got it.

The passage and the picture make you think of life in the frozen lands of the far north.

Here are ten words linked to that part of the world. Make a list of the words in alphabetical order. Then find each word in a dictionary and write down the meaning. Give your list the heading **An Arctic word-list**.

| frost | Eskimo | sledge | blizzard | ski |
| igloo | iceberg | husky | moose | icicle |

Spelling

A   All the words in the list below are from the passage. In each case write down the **verb** the word comes from. The first one is done for you.

> finding – find
> holding
> aching
> riding
> hanging
> sheltering
> moving
> stepping

Did you notice that **four** of the words needed careful spelling, as you could not just add <u>ing</u> to the verb?

B   Here are five more verbs. In each case write down a word ending in <u>ing</u>, formed from the verb. Take care especially with verbs ending in <u>e</u>.

> jump   dive   skip   race   fly

Language

In the passage Swiftly told Alan about the herds of reindeer. The word <u>herd</u> is an example of a **collective noun**. The words <u>flock</u> and <u>team</u> are also collective nouns.

Write out each of the following sentences, putting in suitable **collective nouns**.

1   In the field near Alan's house the farmer keeps a _____ of cows.
2   He sometimes puts a small _____ of sheep in the next field.
3   One day a _____ of boys started to throw stones at the sheep.
4   Suddenly one of the boys noticed a _____ of bees flying towards them.
5   The boys ran away as if they were being chased by a _____ of wolves.

A dreadful mistake

The Court Magician at Incrediblania carefully mixed a watery-looking liquid with a yellow-looking liquid. The result was a lemonade-looking liquid and the most unreasonable smell.

"Ha!" exclaimed the Magician in a rather muffled voice because he had his handkerchief to his nose, owing to the smell.

For ages he had been trying to make an extra specially potent potion. And at last he had succeeded. He poured the potion into a tumbler to let the smell clear away and took it along to lock it safely away in his special cupboard.

On the way he met the Butler, who was taking a glass of lemonade to the King.

"Oh, just a moment if you don't mind," said the Butler, putting down the lemonade. "Would you show me just once more how to make a handkerchief disappear?"

"Why certainly," said the Magician, who had been giving the Butler lessons in magic for simply weeks, but hadn't managed to make him learn much. He put down his glass of potion and showed the Butler how to make the handkerchief disappear. He showed him twenty-seven times and at last the Butler could almost do it.

"Well, I must be off now," said the Magician. "Practise like anything and I'll show you again when I get back from my holidays, if you can't do it by then."

"Thanks frightfully," said the Butler. And then a dreadful thing happened.

The Butler picked up the glass of potent magic potion by mistake, thinking it was a glass of lemonade, and took it to the King; while the Magician carried off the lemonade and locked it carefully away in his cupboard.

Then the Court Magician went for his holiday.

His Majesty picked up the glass and drank off the contents at one go. He was so thirsty he couldn't stop.

"Pwouff!" he said most un-majestically, as he made a face. "What disagreeable lemonade. You must have forgotten to put the sugar in or something."

"More likely he forgot to put the lemon in," said the Queen, whose knitting wouldn't go right, so she felt cross.

Then with a sudden and terrifying *whiz-z-z*, His Majesty the King shrank to only two inches high!

from 'The Home-made Dragon' by Norman Hunter

Understanding

A   Make a list of what you think are the five **main** events of the story.

B   The author of the passage wants to make you laugh. What do you think was **funny** about each of the following?

1   the liquid the Magician made
2   the Butler's attempts to learn the trick with the handkerchief
3   the fact that the Magician went on his holiday
4   the Queen's reply about the lemon
5   the name of the kingdom (see line 1)

My own work

A   Imagine you were the King of Incrediblania. Describe what happened when you found yourself two inches high.

B   Now imagine you were the Magician. Describe what happened when you came back from your holiday.

Bottles like those in the picture and those used by the Court Magician in Incrediblania must be labelled properly. We need to know what liquid is inside the bottle.

Imagine you have to make labels for five bottles like those in the picture. Choose bottles of different shapes and sizes. Make a label to fit each one, writing clearly on the label the name of the liquid it will contain.

Words

A The name of the country, <u>Incrediblania</u>, made you think of the **strange** things that happened there.

Make up interesting or amusing names for the following strange countries.

1 a country where everyone is very small
2 a very happy country
3 a country where it is always very hot
4 a very rich country
5 a country where everyone is very thin

B Now here are five **real** places with interesting names. For each one write a sentence, saying how you think it got its name.

1 Iceland   **4** Golden Gate Bridge
2 Newfoundland   **5** Mount Terror
3 Thunder Bay

Language

A Look at the fourth paragraph of the passage. Notice the way the word <u>who</u> is used, instead of a new sentence beginning with <u>He</u>.

Make each of the following into **one** sentence by using the word <u>who</u>.

1 The Court Magician met the Butler. The Butler was going to see the King.
2 The King was talking to the Queen. She was knitting.
3 The King was angry with the Magician. The Magician could not be found.
4 The Butler told the King and Queen. They were very angry.
5 The King had to be put on the table. He was only two inches high.

B Now write five interesting sentences about people you know. Each sentence should begin "I am writing about _____ _____, who ...."

45

Pippi takes care of herself

There was a time when Pippi had had a father, and she had been very fond of him. Of course, she had had a mother too, but that was long ago.

Pippi's mother had died when Pippi was just a tiny baby lying in her cradle and howling so dreadfully that no one could come near. Pippi believed that her mother now lived somewhere up in Heaven and looked down on her little girl through a hole in it. Pippi often used to wave up to her and say, "Don't worry, I can look after myself!"

Pippi hadn't forgotten her father. He had been a ship's captain, and sailed on the great ocean. Pippi had sailed with him on his boat, at least until the time he had blown into the sea during a storm and disappeared. But Pippi was quite sure that one day he would come back, for she never believed that he had drowned. She was certain that he had come ashore on a desert island, one with lots and lots of cannibals, and that her father had become king of them all and went about all day with a gold crown on his head.

"*My* father is a Cannibal King; there aren't *many* children with so fine a father!" said Pippi, really pleased with herself. "And when my father has built himself a boat he'll come to fetch me, and then *I* shall become a Cannibal Princess. What a life it will be!"

Her father had bought the old cottage in the orchard many years ago. He had wanted to live there with Pippi when he grew old and sailed the seas no longer. But then he had unfortunately been blown into the sea, and as Pippi expected him to return she went straight home to Villekulla Cottage, as their house was called. It stood there furnished and ready and waiting for her. One fine summer's evening she had said good-bye to all the sailors on her father's boat. They liked Pippi very much, and Pippi liked them.

"Good-bye, boys!" said Pippi, kissing each in turn on the forehead. "Don't worry about me. I can take care of myself!"

from 'Pippi Longstocking' by Astrid Lindgren

Understanding

A   1   What did Pippi remember about her father?
       2   What did she hope had happened to her father?
       3   What did she think had happened to her mother?
       4   Why do you think the sailors liked Pippi so much?
       5   What does the last sentence tell you about Pippi?

B   Make a list of what you think were the five most important moments of Pippi's life, that are mentioned in the passage.

My own work

A   Imagine Pippi's father **was** still alive, and sent her a letter describing what had happened to him. Write the letter he sent.

B   Now write Pippi's answer, telling her father what **she** had been doing.

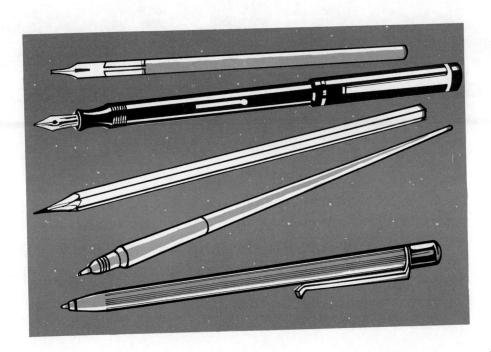

If Pippi Longstocking had lived many years ago she might have sailed with her father in a sailing ship like the one in the picture.

Many parts of a ship have special words to describe them. Make a tracing of the sailing ship in the picture and then neatly label your picture with the following words.

bow   stern   mast   sails   deck

48

Spelling

Look at the sentence near the end of the passage that begins 'One fine summer's evening ....' In this sentence are two **nouns** that name people (<u>sailor</u> and <u>father</u>.) We have to learn the endings of nouns like these, which end in <u>er</u> or <u>or</u>.

Here are ten sentences to complete. The missing words end in <u>er</u> or <u>or</u>. The first letter of each missing word is given. Check your answers in a dictionary.

1   Pippi's m_____ died when Pippi was a baby.
2   When you are ill you sometimes need a d_____.
3   If you are a good s_____ you might be in a choir.
4   When you buy meat you usually buy it from a b_____.
5   Many buses have a c_____ to collect the fares.
6   Sometimes an i_____ gets on the bus, to check everyone has a ticket.
7   When you buy something from a shop you become a c_____.
8   A man who takes part in a play is called an a_____.
9   You have to learn to be a good g_____ if you want to grow flowers and vegetables.
10   The a_____ of the passage is Astrid Lindgren.

Language

Look at the fourth paragraph of the passage. In the second half of the paragraph Pippi said ".......... <u>he'll come</u> to fetch me, and then <u>I shall become</u> a Cannibal Princess. What a life it <u>will be</u>."

She was thinking about the future and the three **verbs** are in the **future tense**. In this tense it is better to use <u>shall</u> rather than <u>will</u> after the word <u>I</u>.

Complete each of the following sentences, in each case including a verb in the **future tense**.

1   When school finishes today all the children ....
2   Next weekend I ....
3   On my next birthday I .... years old.
4   The next school I go to ....
5   I hope the weather tomorrow ....

unit 12

A gentle dragon

Out of the cave came a green, scaly foot, well furnished with claws. Sue stepped back a little. It was safer to be near the rocks, she thought. Another foot appeared, and above it a large head, long like a horse's head, but bright green in colour and shining like glass. The creature had two ears and a pair of golden-yellow horns, very highly polished. His eyes were large and yellow too, like gleaming lamps. He did not look at all frightening. He seemed to have no teeth, and his wide, wide mouth was set in a charming smile.

"Shall I come out any further?" he asked.

"Well," began Sue, and hesitated.

"I promise I won't eat you," said the dragon. "I never eat anyone nowadays. I've quite changed my habits."

"Well," said Susan again. "I'd love to see your tail. Have you got a long one?"

The dragon turned slowly round, and Susan could see his scaly back, along the top of which were rows of yellow fins, rather like a fish's, only much bigger, and then he slowly uncoiled several yards of emerald green tail, decorated with yellow scales arranged in patterns. Laid close against his back, tidily folded, were his wings, which, like his tail, were green and scaly, and patterned with gold.

"Now are you sure I'm a dragon?" he said, and his voice sounded impatient.

"Oh, yes," said Susan. "I'm quite sure now. You couldn't be anything else. Why were you sneezing? Have you got a bad cold?"

"Well," answered the dragon, "I'll tell you. I often find bits of food left over by picnic parties, and eat them up for breakfast or supper – paste sandwiches, shrimps, apples, jam turnovers – little things like that, you know. And last night I found a bag with a hard-boiled egg in it, and a lot of eggshells. I thought I'd have it for breakfast, but when I opened the bag, I found that the horrid people had left lots of salt and pepper in it as well, and it got up my nose and made me sneeze."

from 'Green Smoke' by Rosemary Manning

50

Understanding

A   **1** Why do you think Sue <u>stepped back a little</u> when the foot came out of the cave?

      2 Why do you think the dragon <u>did not look at all frightening</u>?

      3 What do you think the dragon meant when he said, "I've quite <u>changed my habits</u>."?

      4 Why do you think the dragon's voice <u>sounded impatient</u> when he said, "Now are you sure I'm a dragon?"?

      5 Why was the dragon <u>sneezing</u>?

B   A very full description of the dragon is given in the passage. Make a list of each part of its body and the words used to describe each part.

My own work

A   You have looked closely at the description of the dragon in the passage. Imagine you met another strange animal that does not really exist. Write a description of the animal you met.

B   Now write a description of any **real** animal that you think is fierce or frightening. It may be best to choose an animal you have actually seen, or seen in pictures.

The animal in the picture is real. Perhaps it looks rather like a dragon, although not like the one described in the passage!

If you look up the word <u>dragon</u> in a dictionary you will read something like this:

dragon: an imaginary animal with scales, wings and sharp teeth, that is supposed to breathe fire.

Here are five more imaginary creatures. Write down how you think a dictionary would describe each one. Then compare your descriptions with those in a dictionary.

elf   mermaid   unicorn   vampire   leprechaun

52

Punctuation

In the last paragraph of the passage there is a list of food left behind by picnic parties: '. . . paste sandwiches, shrimps, apples, jam turnovers.' Commas are used to separate the items in the list.

Complete the following sentences, including in each case a list of objects. Make sure you use commas correctly.

1 When I emptied the litter basket I found ....
2 On a shelf in the supermarket were ....
3 In my toy cupboard I used to keep ....
4 At dinner-time I put on the table ....
5 From the window of this room I can see ....

Language

A   Inverted commas "..........." are used to show the actual words spoken by somebody in a story. Look at the passage again and complete these sentences.

1 The dragon started a new speech _____ times.
2 Sue started a new speech _____ times.
3 Each time the speaker changed the writer began a new _____.
4 Only the actual words spoken were put inside _____ _____.
5 The dragon's first speech was a question. The question mark was placed _____ the inverted commas.

B   Imagine you are having a conversation with a new friend who asks you five questions about yourself. Write out the conversation, making sure you use inverted commas correctly.

On the beach after a storm

The boys were wearing oilskins and sea-boots. Gildas had a new sweater of unbleached wool, that still had a faint smell of sheep. It tickled his neck rather badly, so he stopped and had a good scratch.

"Let's look for things," said Vonik.

The great joy of the beach after a storm was the things that had been washed up. They never knew what they would find. One day, they might find treasure, but, in the meantime, the things that they found were almost as good.

Today the beach was strewn with driftwood and broken lobster pots. There was a tangle of blue fishing net that had been torn loose by the gale. They left that for the fishermen. Next they found a bicycle wheel. Why had that been in the sea? Then they found a plastic bottle that had once contained shampoo, and a rather rusty toy car. There were three big glass floats from a fishing net. They were lovely and smooth to touch, and strange and cloudy to look into. They left those too for the fishermen. Then they found a small knife, in good condition. The blade, which was very sharp, curved up at the end.

"It's a strange sort of dagger," said Gildas.

"It's a ship's cook's knife for chopping herbs," said Vonik.

Next came a string of beads, which had been in the water a long time. They were covered with weed, and tiny shellfish had settled themselves to live there. Near it was a book, too sodden to read, and a torn sunshade. After that they found a metal mould, shaped like a castle, with turrets and battlements. They scooped out the sand and seaweed that was packed inside it, and filled it with clean, fresh sand. They patted it down with their hands, and then carefully turned the mould upside down. A perfect miniature castle stood before them. Very carefully, so as not to break it, they put tiny shells for the doors and a flag of seaweed to fly from the tower.

"It's a jelly-mould really," said Vonik. He knew all about such things, for his mother was the best cook for miles around.

from 'The Edge of the World' by Jacynth Hope-Simpson

Understanding

A 1 What sort of clothes were the boys wearing?
   2 What was exciting about visiting the beach after the storm?
   3 Why did the boys think the things they found were almost as good as treasure?
   4 Who else did they expect to visit the beach to see what they could find?
   5 How did Vonik recognise the knife for chopping herbs and the jelly mould?

B   Make two lists of the things the boys found on the beach. In the first list put the things you think they would normally expect to find there. In the second list put the things you think surprised them. Give each list a suitable heading.

My own work

A   Imagine **you** visited the beach after a storm and found some interesting objects. Write a paragraph about **five** of the objects you found.

      Begin your paragraph, 'The first thing I found was ....'

B   Finding things is just one of the activities you can do on a beach. Describe **one** other activity on the beach that is also very popular.

The picture shows men digging on a beach like the one Gildas and Vonik visited. The men are probably looking for small creatures they can use as bait to catch fish.

Here are the names of five creatures that are found on the shore or in the sea.

crab   cockle   lobster   lugworm   starfish

Use an encyclopaedia to find out more about these creatures and for each one write down the information you think is important.

Sentences

Look at the sentence, near the end of the passage, that says, 'After that they found a metal mould, shaped like a castle, with turrets and battlements.' This sentence **describes the mould** and the rest of the paragraph **describes what the boys did with it**. Altogether there are **five** sentences about the metal mould.

Choose one of the **other** objects the boys found and write a paragraph of five sentences about it. The first sentence should describe the object and the other four should describe what you think the boys did with it.

Language

In Unit 7 there was a question on beginning sentences with good short **phrases**.

Here are ten more short phrases, all connected with the seaside. Complete each sentence in an interesting way, to tell a story about a visit to the seaside by Gildas and Vonik. The first one is done for you.

1 On the beach Gildas and Vonik built a fort with huge sandcastles.
2 In the sand ....
3 Among the rocks ....
4 In the sky ....
5 At the bottom of the cliffs ....
6 On the pier ....
7 In the amusement centre ....
8 At a stall in the market ....
9 In the café ....
10 On the way home ....

Hurry Home

You had better hurry home for your supper's nearly ready,
Your mother's in the kitchen and she's awfully wild,
She's been shouting at the cat, and she keeps on saying,
"O where has he got to, the wretched child?"

She has been to the front door and looked through the window
And now she's banging on the frying-pan,
The plates and the dishes are all on the table,
So run, my boy, as fast as you can.

Don't you know she's cooking your favourite supper,
Potatoes in their jackets and beefsteak pie?
She's made a jug of custard for the pudding in the oven,
Get a move on, Joe, the stars are in the sky.

They've all left the factory, the streets will soon be empty,
No more playing now, it's time you fed,
It really is a shame to keep your mother waiting,
So come have your supper, and then off to bed.

Leonard Clark

Understanding

A Write down **five** things Joe's mother does to show she is angry or upset.

B Write down **five** reasons the poem suggests that it is time Joe went home.

My own work

A Joe obviously likes to play out after school. Think back over the last five school days and write about what you did each day between leaving school and going to bed. Write your account like a diary.

B When Joe eventually arrives home his favourite supper is waiting for him. Describe **your** favourite meal.

The picture and the poem are both concerned with kitchens. There are certain things you would expect to find in most kitchens. Make a list of the ten most important things you would include in a new kitchen. Give your list the heading **Kitchen equipment.**

Words

A   In the first line of the poem the poet has used <u>supper's</u> instead of <u>supper is</u>, to help the rhythm of the line. There are **ten** places in the poem where the poet has used an **apostrophe** for the same reason. Make a list of the ten words, beginning <u>supper's</u> = <u>supper is</u>.

B   When people are talking they often use **abbreviations** like <u>supper's</u>. Write out each of the following sentences, using abbreviations instead of the words underlined.

1   When <u>breakfast is</u> ready <u>I shall</u> get up.
2   My favourite <u>cereal is</u> corn flakes.
3   Now <u>it is</u> time to go to school.
4   My <u>friend is</u> waiting and <u>I had</u> better hurry up.
5   <u>There will</u> be a nice tea waiting when <u>school is</u> over.

Language

A   Look at the word <u>shouting</u> in the third line of the poem. Words ending in <u>ing</u> are usually formed from **verbs**. In this case <u>shouting</u> is formed from the verb <u>shout</u>. As we saw in Unit 9 we have to spell these words carefully.

There are seven more words ending in <u>ing</u> in the poem. Six of them are formed from verbs. Write down these six words and in each case write down the verb from which the word is formed.

B   Here is a story about Joe, the boy in the poem. Write out the story, using interesting words ending in <u>ing</u> in the ten gaps.

One evening, when Joe was _____ in the garden, he heard someone _____ from the house across the road. When he looked at the house, he thought he could see a red glow _____ from one of the upstairs windows. _____ that something was wrong, he ran into his house _____ for his mother who was _____ in the kitchen. _____ that there was a fire, she dialled 999. The firemen soon arrived and the neighbour who had been trapped was saved by _____ down a ladder. Later Joe was rewarded for _____ such good sense and _____ someone's life.

61

An unexpected visit

Peter and Richard were sitting on the rocks looking into the rock pool. Their legs were dangling into the pool. Peter's legs were longer, so the water came half-way up them.

He felt about with his toes under a large rock. He could feel the ridges in the rock and some seaweed that seemed to flutter when he touched it. But he couldn't discover the ridgy shells he was probing for.

The bottom of Richard's feet only just reached the surface of the water. He was patting it with his feet, making ripples and turning the water cloudy.

Peter and Richard had already filled a bucket with limpets and seaweed and sea water to take home. Peter had a tank there with sea water in it and he liked collecting things for it. Each time their father took them to a beach they collected a few mollusc shells and seaweed.

"Look," said Richard, suddenly. "Whatever's that, Pete? Out at sea. A porpoise – it might be. Or a seal – or perhaps a whale?"

"There aren't any seals around this bay," said Peter. "At least, I don't *think* so."

Peter knew about fish and animals and insects. He was always finding out more about them from his encyclopaedia, which had coloured pictures in it. "I don't *think* there are any nearer than Cornwall." He was prodding the seaweed.

"Well, do *look* then," said Richard. "It must be a whale. It's getting bigger and coming up higher – just round by the point where those rocks sticking out look like a lion's head."

Peter looked up from the rock pool. "Goodness," he said, and chewed his lips. "It's – yes! It's a submarine!"

Richard got out the binoculars his uncle had given him for Christmas. He usually watched gulls through them. But this was much bigger than a gull. "You can see the name painted on its side!"

"Let's see," said Peter, borrowing the glasses. "It's the sub's name." He spelled it. "A-G-A-M-E-M-N-O-N. Agamemnon."

"What's that mean?" asked Richard.

"It's the name of one of those men in the Greek stories."

"Oh!" said Richard. "It's a very long name. Silly to give it such a long name if the sailors have to paint all those letters on the side."

"On the hull, you mean," said Peter, who knew a bit about boats, too.

from "Richard's M-Class Cows" by P. D. Pemberton

● Understanding

Using clues from the passage, answer these questions. In each case explain **why** you chose that answer.

1 What time of year was it?
2 Were Peter and Richard brothers, cousins or friends?
3 Who was the taller of the two?
4 Had the boys been playing near the pool for a long time?
5 Was this the first time they had been to the coast?
6 How did Peter know so much about so many things?
7 What was the submarine doing when they spotted it?
8 Why did Richard mistake the submarine for animals that live in the sea?
9 Were the boys surprised to see a submarine?
10 Where would Peter say you would find the name of a ship?

● My own work

Imagine that Peter and Richard hid behind the rocks as the submarine came nearer. Write an exciting story about what happened next.

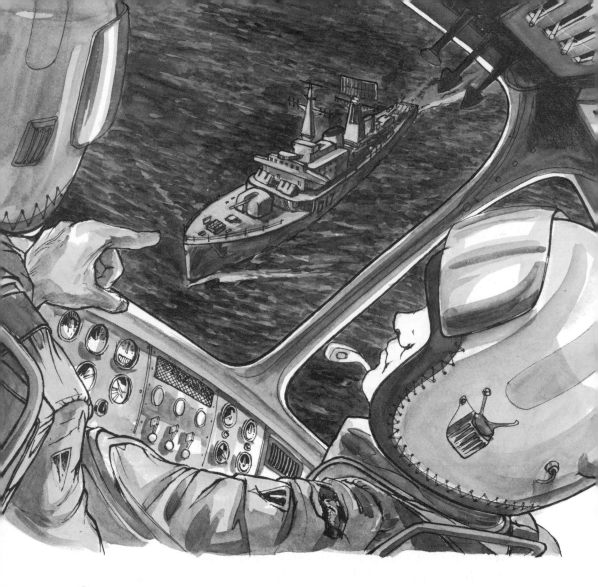

The ship in the picture and the submarine described in the passage might become famous. Some ships are **very** famous. Use an encyclopaedia to find out information about each of these famous ships.

Golden Hind   Mayflower   Victory   Titanic   QE2

Write down the name of each ship and write a few notes about each one to show why it was so famous. Give your work the heading **Famous ships.**

Words

A   A submarine is one type of boat or ship. Here are the names of ten more types of boat or ship. For each one write a sentence that explains what it is like or what it is used for.

barge	ferry
canoe	launch
yacht	lifeboat
liner	raft
trawler	tanker

B   The submarine in the passage was called <u>Agamemnon</u>. Every boat or ship has a name. Imagine you could give a name to each of the boats or ships listed in Part A of this question. Write out the list of boats or ships and opposite each one put the name you would choose.

Language

A   Look at the word <u>submarine</u>. <u>Marine</u> tells us that the word is connected with <u>the sea</u>, while the first part of the word, <u>sub</u>, means <u>under</u>. So a <u>submarine</u> goes <u>under the sea</u>.

The first part of the word, <u>sub</u>, is called a **prefix**. Another common prefix is <u>tele</u>, meaning <u>from a long way</u>.

Here are five more words that use prefixes. Write down each word and what you think the word and the prefix mean. Use a dictionary to check your answers.

    television   disappear   unusual
        semi-circle   pre-historic

B   Now find each of the following words in the dictionary and write down what each word and its prefix mean.

    automatic   nonsense   postpone
        supersonic   tricycle

65

Surprises in the garden

Ann and Roger had never seen a real sundial before, and Ann had to be shown how it worked, and Roger, who had read all about sundials in a book, showed her. Then they bent over the base of the pedestal. The lettering was old and crumbly and hard to read, but Roger finally made it out.

"It says . . ." He broke off and looked at the others. "It says 'Anything Can Happen!' "

"That isn't all," said Anne, who had wandered round to the back of the sundial. "The lettering goes on, round here. It says . . ." She leaned over to make out the final words. "It says, 'Anything Can Happen When You've All the Time in the World!' "

"What did I tell you?" Eliza's eyes were glowing now. "That old Mrs. Whiton sent us here on purpose! She's probably a witch! It all connects! It's true! I feel it in my bones! Anything *could* happen here! Something probably *will* any minute!"

As she spoke something flashed through the air and disappeared in the grass at their feet.

"What was that?" said Ann.

"It came from the sundial," said Roger. "Something live must have been sitting there, and then it hopped off."

"There it goes!" said Jack, pointing through the opening in the hedge.

"Come on!" said Eliza.

The four children raced through the opening after the hopping thing. Then they stopped short.

From where they stood a bank led down to the sea, and the bank was all covered with little flat creeping plants that flowed over rock ledges and turned boulders to flowery cushions, for the plants were studded all over with tiny starry blossoms, purple and lavender and white. The smell of the bank was like all the sweetness and spice of the world mixed together. And it was here that the innumerable bees hummed.

The thing they were following gave another hop and landed just ahead of them. *"There* it is!" said Ann.

"Never mind it, it's just an old toad," said Eliza. "What's all this wonderful smelly stuff?" And she threw herself down on its redolent pillowiness, and the others followed her example.

"It smells like turkey stuffing," said Jack.

"It's some kind of herb," said Roger. He tasted one of the tiny dark-green leaves of the purple-flowering kind. "I think maybe it's thyme."

from 'The Time Garden' by Edward Eager

● Understanding

A   What do you think is most interesting about each of the following?

> the sundial
> Eliza
> Mrs. Whiton
> the toad
> the bank that led down to the sea

B   Now imagine you had to make up a question for other children to answer about each of the people or things listed in Part A of this question. Write out the questions you would ask.

● My own work

Write out the saying that went round the sundial described in the passage. Imagine **you** had all the time in the world. What would you like to do?

The picture and the passage make you think of gardens. Here are five headings about trees, bushes, plants and flowers.

1 Flowers that bloom in the spring
2 Flowers of different colours
3 Trees and bushes that bear tasty fruit
4 Trees that are very common
5 My favourite plants

Write down one of the headings, underline it and then make a list of five names that fit the heading. Do the same with each of the other headings. You may wish to use some names more than once.

Give the whole piece of work a suitable title.

Handwriting

Here are ten more **sayings** or **proverbs** like the one on the sundial. Write each one out in your best handwriting, say it to yourself and think about its meaning.

1 Better late than never.
2 More haste less speed.
3 It takes two to make a quarrel.
4 Last but not least.
5 Too many cooks spoil the broth.
6 Look before you leap.
7 In at one ear and out at the other.
8 A stitch in time saves nine.
9 One good turn deserves another.
10 A fool and his money are soon parted.

Language

Look again at the saying on the sundial. Notice that it has **inverted commas** or **quotation marks** around it. These are used for sayings, titles and quotations, as well as for the words people speak in stories.

Here are ten sentences to complete. Make sure you use quotation marks correctly.

1 The saying on the sundial was ....
2 The saying or proverb I like best is ....
3 Another saying or proverb I know is ....
4 My favourite book is ....
5 My favourite television programme is ....
6 The best film I have ever seen was ....
7 The title of my favourite song is ....
8 When Jack was talking in the passage about the smell of the plants, he said ....
9 The title of the passage is ....
10 The title of this book is ....

Cleaning up the old railway

The carriage was very dusty and dirty and it smelt somehow unused, but it was also a good deal warmer and less draughty than the booking office and there were, of course, a great many comfortable seats. Sue plumped down on one of them and then sneezed violently as a cloud of dust flew up around her. She half shut her eyes and bounced up and down pretending that she was travelling very fast through a foreign country.

In the distance she could hear the boys both talking at once, the clinking noise made by the spade against the rails and then a very rusty, clanking sound followed by cries of triumph.

"Undone one of their old points I suppose," said Sue to herself, "well I'd better get on if I want to surprise them and there's a lot to be done."

Within a very few minutes the dust was swirling out of the carriage and Ellie, who had come hopping over the lines to investigate, retreated hurriedly with an angry 'tck-tck-tck-TCK'.

It was nearly two hours after this that Barny could resist the truly awful pangs of hunger no longer and called a halt for food.

"Couldn't we just grease up the points?" asked Andy, whose face, in spite of the cold wind, was almost as red as his hair from hard work.

"Nope," said Barny firmly. "I want my dinner!"

Andy stacked their tools neatly and was about to follow Barny across the line towards the station when a carriage door swung open and Sue's extremely dusty face appeared.

"Your food's in here," she called. "I've got yours too, Andy. I brought over your lunch box."

"What are you doing there?" Andy asked.

"Working, same as you. I've been here nearly all the morning, only you were banging and talking such a lot you didn't notice. I walked right past you twice. Oh come *on*," Sue swung out even further in her impatience, "I want you to see what I've done."

She had done a great deal and the boys were generous enough to say so for the carriage, although still shabby, was now dirt and dust free and smelt pleasantly of polish.

from 'The Secret Railway' by Elisabeth Beresford

Understanding

1 Imagine that Sue was keeping a diary. Write out what she put in the diary about the morning she spent cleaning the carriage.
2 Now do the same for **either** Andy **or** Barny about the way **they** spent the morning.
3 What do you think Sue would be most pleased about?
4 What do you think Andy or Barny would be most pleased about?
5 How do the first and last sentences of the passage help to show how well the children had worked?

My own work

A Imagine it began to rain while the children were having their lunch and they had to stay in the carriage all afternoon. Describe what work they did in the carriage and the games they played.

B Look at the last sentence of the first paragraph. Imagine you were Sue. Where would you be travelling and what would you be pretending?

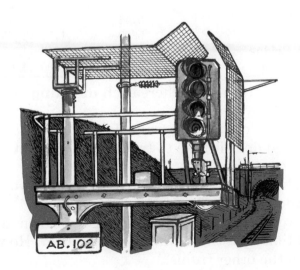

When you travel by train you have to be able to read a **timetable**. Here is an example of one. Notice it uses the 24-hour clock. For example 1 p.m. is shown as 1300. When you have studied the timetable answer the questions below.

name of station	time of departure				
Newtown	0725	0940	1120	1420	1700
Market Bray	0745	—	1140	1440	1720
Ludderton	0800	—	1155	1455	1735
Carlton Bridge	0845	—	1240	1540	1820
Slade-by-Sea	0905	1100	1300	1600	1840

1 How many trains are there each **morning** between Newtown and Slade-by-Sea?
2 What time does the last train of the day arrive in Slade-by-Sea?
3 How long does it take to travel from Market Bray to Carlton Bridge?
4 If you lived in Ludderton which train would you catch to arrive in Slade-by-Sea before 4.15 p.m?
5 One train travels non-stop from Newtown to Slade-by-Sea. What time does this train leave Newtown? How much faster is it than the other trains?

Spelling

The words <u>a lot</u> occur twice in the passage. Write out the sentences in which they occur. It is important to remember that we write <u>a lot</u> as two words, **not** one.

All the following need careful spelling. Some of them consist of **one** word and some are **two** words. Use each one in a sentence about yourself and learn the correct spelling.

a bit	sometimes
in fact	myself
all right	cannot
no one	everybody
in case	upstairs

Language

Look at the word <u>warmer</u> in the first sentence of the passage. It **makes a comparison** between the carriage and the booking office.

<u>Warm</u> is an **adjective**. We use <u>warmer</u> instead of saying <u>more warm</u>. We call <u>warmer</u> the **comparative of** <u>warm</u>.

Here are ten more adjectives. In each case write down the comparative. The words in the right-hand column need special care.

old	happy
brave	good
small	beautiful
black	naughty
hot	bad

The strange man who lived in a cave

After breakfast Barney slipped out of the house and went off to the pit. In the copse the frozen leaves crunched like cornflakes under his feet. He climbed down into the pit on the far side, where the cliff was lowest, and it hurt his fingers to hold on to the icy tree roots. The nettles were all dead in the bottom of the pit and the old cans had lumps of solid ice in them.

There was no sign of life in the shelter, though he noticed the ashes of a small dead fire and a faint smell of wood-smoke still hung around. But at the back of the cave was a kind of nest made of bracken and dead grass and newspaper. He thought he heard breathing sounds coming out of it.

"Stig!" Barney called. Nothing happened. "I wonder if he's like a dormouse," he thought, "and goes to sleep all the winter."

He called again. "Stig! Are you there?"

There was a rustle in the nest, and a mop of black hair poked up out of it. Underneath it was Stig's face, but it was screwed up in a very strange expression.

"Is he cross?" wondered Barney anxiously.

His eyes still screwed up and his mouth shut, Stig took a deep breath.

Then he sneezed. It was a sneeze like a cannon going off, and it made the cave echo.

"You did give me a fright!" said Barney. "You've got a cold, Stig. No wonder, when you live in this damp place. You need a good fire."

He looked around the shelter and the cave. There didn't seem to be any wood to burn. Stig's heavy flint axe was leaning against the wall and Barney picked it up, but he saw that the edge was crumbled and blunt.

"You'll have to sharpen this," said Barney.

Stig crawled out of his nest, blinking stupidly. He moved as if his joints were rusty and he did not take the axe as Barney held it out to him.

"All right, I'll do it then," said Barney. "I expect it's quite easy."

from 'Stig of the Dump' by Clive King

Understanding

1 Why do you think Barney <u>slipped</u> out of the house?
2 Write down **two** ways the first paragraph shows how cold it was.
3 What did Barney find in the cave that told him someone was living there?
4 Why did Barney compare Stig with a dormouse?
5 Why did Barney think Stig might be cross?
6 What was actually the matter with Stig?
7 What did Barney decide to do to help Stig?
8 Why did Barney's plan become difficult?
9 What have you learned about Barney from the passage?
10 What have you learned about Stig from the passage?

My own work

Look again at the first sentence of the passage. Think of some time when **you** had an adventure and make up a story about it, beginning in the same interesting way as the passage:

After _____ I slipped out of the house and went off to ....

Perhaps Stig's cave had **stalactites** and **stalagmites** like the cave above. Look up the two words in a dictionary to find out what they are and what the difference is between them. Which of the two words came first in the dictionary? Notice that it was the **sixth** letter of the words that told you the correct alphabetical order.

At the top of each page in most dictionaries you will find the first and last words shown on that page. We use these two words to tell us if the word we are looking for is on that page **or** earlier **or** later.

1   Put these words in alphabetical order.

   sparkle   starling   shoulder   scoop   spark
   steady   soldier   starboard   solid   scream

2   Imagine a page in a dictionary had at the top the two words **snow** and **squirrel**. Which of the words in question **1** would be found on that page? Which would come on an earlier page? Which would come later?

76

Words

In the passage there were two interesting comparisons. In the first paragraph the frozen leaves were compared with the crunch of cornflakes. Later Stig's sneeze was compared with a cannon going off.

Here are ten sentences to complete with interesting comparisons.

1 In the middle of the night the wind sounded like ....
2 My baby sister's crying sounded like ....
3 The noise of her rattle was like ....
4 The material of my new coat felt like ....
5 On my way to school the rain felt like ....
6 The polish on the classroom floor smelled like ....
7 The noise in the playground was like ....
8 The smell from the kitchen was like ....
9 When it went dark the street lights looked like ....
10 When everyone was asleep the quiet was like ....

Language

A   In Units 7 and 13 we looked at the use of short **phrases**. These phrases often begin with words like <u>after</u>, <u>of</u>, <u>to</u>, <u>in</u>, <u>under</u>. These words are called **prepositions.**

Read the first two sentences of the passage again and write down the phrases that begin with the five prepositions listed above.

B   Now look at the end of the passage and write a short paragraph of three or four sentences to add to the end. Underline any **prepositions** that you use.

A magician from the 11th century visits the 20th century

Catweazle woke very early the next morning hearing a strange noise in the sky. The hair stood up on his dirty neck as it came nearer, and finally, when the thunderous noise was overhead he could bear it no longer, and, darting out of the chicken coop he looked up and saw a huge fish swimming across the sky. Its fins were motionless, and it roared so loudly that the earth shook.

As it passed over him, Catweazle flung himself down in the wet grass and waited for it to pounce, but the giant creature was apparently not hungry and it continued on its way until it disappeared in the distance. It was Catweazle's first aeroplane.

He rose unsteadily and began to creep towards the farm, hiding quickly as he saw Mr. Bennet and Winston moving between the sheds. Still shaken by the aeroplane, he was making his way along the wall of the garage when he heard another strange sound, this time like the hissing of serpents. Curiosity overcoming his fear, he looked round the open door.

It was Barakiel! The Prince of Lightning! As the Demon turned his great head, revealing his one monstrous eye, showers of little stars tumbled from his blasting rod.

Catweazle jerked back making tiny cries of fear and a curious fizzing noise through his teeth. He turned and fled from the garage.

Sam Woodyard turned off the welder, and, lifting his protective helmet, caught a glimpse of Catweazle running towards the back door of the farmhouse.

Carrot, who was at the sink in the scullery, suddenly saw Catweazle coming up to the house and quickly pulled the old man inside. Catweazle was in such a panic of fear that he ran past Carrot into the kitchen and went to earth under the table.

"Oh, Master, Master," he moaned as Carrot ran in after him, "deliver me from the Demon." Getting a lump of chalk from a pocket in his tattered robe, he drew a circle round himself on the flagstones.

"Sator, Arepo, Tenet, Opera, Rotas," he muttered.

"Get up," said Carrot, who was expecting his father at any moment.

"Gab, gaba, agaba."

"Will you get up?" ordered the boy, hauling him out. "You've got me into enough trouble already. If Dad finds you, he'll skin you alive."

from 'Catweazle' by Richard Carpenter

Understanding

1   Catweazle had never seen an aeroplane before. Read the first two paragraphs again and write down **three** thoughts that you think went through his mind when he saw and heard it.

2   Write down **three** thoughts that you think went through his mind when he saw Sam Woodyard using the welder. (A welder is used to heat pieces of metal so that they will melt and then can be joined together.)

3   Why do you think Catweazle was so frightened by the aeroplane and the welder?

4   What did Catweazle do to save himself from each of them?

5   How did Carrot, a boy who was trying to help Catweazle, deal with him?

My own work

It was very frightening for someone from the 11th century to find himself in the 20th century. Think of **three** more things that Catweazle might have met for the first time. Describe what happened in each case. Make sure you describe the object first as Catweazle saw it **before** you say what it really was.

●   The picture shows someone using a welder like the one that frightened Catweazle.

Imagine there was a notice on the wall behind the welder, headed **Safety precautions**. Make an eye-catching notice for the wall, listing five instructions on how to use the welder safely.

Now make another notice, for the wall of your classroom, about crossing the road safely. Base your notice on the Green Cross Code.

Words

When Catweazle hid under the table in the kitchen he said a spell to save himself from the Demon. If the words are written down they make a magic word square that can be read from left to right, from right to left, from top to bottom and from bottom to top. (The strange words are actually Latin.)

S	A	T	O	R
A	R	E	P	O
T	E	N	E	T
O	P	E	R	A
R	O	T	A	S

A   Here is a simple word square for you to make. Answer these questions and you should have a word square with three **three-letter** words.
   1   What is the number after nine?
   2   Who was the wife of Adam?
   3   What do you have to hit the ball over in tennis?

B   Now make a magic word square of your own.

Language

Look at the first sentence of the second paragraph of the passage. The word <u>passed</u> comes from the verb <u>pass</u>.

Now look at the sentence, near the end of the passage, which describes how Catweazle hid under the table. In it you will see the word <u>past</u>. This word has the same **pronunciation** as <u>passed</u> but a very different **meaning**.

Here is a story about the seaside. In **ten** places you are given two words and have to choose the correct one. Write out the story putting in what you think are the right words. Check your answers in the dictionary.

One day we went by train to the seaside. The **fair/fare** was not too **dear/deer.** We spent most of the day on the **beach/beech** where we watched a boat with a huge many-coloured **sail/sale.** It was a beautiful **sight/site** and one I wanted to **stair/stare** at all day. It **made/maid** the **hole/whole** world seem at **peace/piece.** How I wished I could have been on **board/bored** that boat.

81

The Silent Spinney

What's that rustling behind me?
Only a cat.
Thank goodness for that,
For I'm afraid of the darkness,
And these tall trees
Are silent and black,
And if ever I get out of here, mate,
I can tell you I'm not coming back.

There's a dark shadow out in the roadway,
See if there's someone behind that tree,
For I'm afraid of the darkness
And it might jump out at me.

My sisters are scared stiff of spiders,
My mother is frightened of mice,
But I'm afraid of the darkness,
I'm not coming this way twice.

Seamus Redmond

Understanding

1 What sort of place does the poem describe?
2 One line in the first verse is repeated almost exactly in each of the other two verses. Which line is it? Why do you think the poet has used it three times?
3 Choose three other things that frighten the poet. In each case explain why he is frightened.
4 What things frighten the poet's mother and sisters? Why do you think the poet mentions them?
5 What does the last line of the poem tell you about the poet?

My own work

A Everyone is frightened from time to time. Make a list of the **things** that frighten you, like spiders or mice. Try to explain why you are frightened by each of them.

B Now describe something that **happened** to you and made you frightened.

The word <u>eerie</u> would be a suitable adjective to describe the **atmosphere** of both the room in the picture and the wood in the poem. Here are nine more adjectives that describe the atmosphere of places.

bleak   gloomy   wild   quaint   solemn
majestic   mysterious   lively   peaceful

Put all ten words in alphabetical order. Find each word in a dictionary and write down its meaning. Give your word-list the heading **Adjectives of atmosphere.**

● Sentences

A   Look at the first two lines of the poem. They consist of a **question** (with **question mark**) and an **answer**.

Here are five **questions** to answer. In each case write down the question and beneath it the answer.

1   What frightens you most of all?
2   What makes you very happy?
3   What makes you angry?
4   Where is the loneliest place you know?
5   Where is the friendliest place you know?

B   Now here are five **answers**, all about trees. In each case make up a question to fit the answer.

1   an area with many trees
2   in spring
3   in the top of a tree
4   a tree that keeps its leaves all year round
5   woodpeckers and squirrels

● Language

A   1   This, that, these and those are useful words. Three of them are used in the poem but one is not. Which is the one that is not used?
2   Which of the four words are singular? Which are plural?
3   Which of the four words refer to things that are near? Which refer to things that are further away?
4   Why do you think the poet used these and not those in line 5?
5   Why do you think the poet used that and not this in line 10?

B   Complete each of the following sentences with the correct word from this, that, these and those.

1   _____ year we are hoping to go to France for our holiday.
2   Last year we went to Cornwall. _____ was the best holiday I've ever had.
3   We brought back _____ shells over there.
4   I also bought _____ bracelet on my arm.
5   _____ are the photographs I took during the holiday.

Finding out about the countryside

Ben got up and wandered out of the gate and into the road. The old lady they called Nosey Parker, who had appeared so often when they were moving into their new house, came out of her front door.

"On your own?" she asked, which was a stupid question, and she put out her hand, almost as if she wanted to stop him.

"I'm getting *measles*," said Ben. Nosey Parker jumped back like a frightened bird. "The others are *terribly* ill. It's a very bad sort of measles, you know," he said. "Even if I breathed like this – poof –", he blew at her, "you'd catch it."

Nosey Parker shot back into her cottage and Ben ran away, up the road and on and on, as fast as he could go, until he came to the Water Meadows. He went through the gate and down the slope to the river where the grass was white with ladysmock. It was boggy here, and he jumped from tussock to tussock until he came to the squidgy river bank, trodden down by cows. On the other side, the June grass was thick and tall. It would be fun to make tracks through it, he thought, and he waded across the shallow river, squelching out the other side with wet sandals.

He crawled through the grass, which waved above his head. Some small creature had made a little track which he followed, parting the grass carefully in case he should surprise the animal and hurt it. He thought he heard a rustle and stopped to listen, but there was only the hiccuping call of a cuckoo. ("In June she changes her tune," he murmured quietly to himself.) He did so much want to see a rabbit or a weasel or a mouse. Ever since they had moved from the town, two weeks ago, he had watched and waited but just as he was sure something was going to come out of the bushes, one of the others made a noise and spoiled everything. Sometimes he would have given anything to be an only child. It was so difficult to get away from the others. This was his big chance. Tomorrow, the measle germs, like a swarm of angry bees, might surround him and stick their invisible swords into him.

from 'Ben's Expedition' by Griselda Gifford

Understanding

What have you learned from the passage about each of the following?

1 the old lady's nickname
2 Ben's behaviour to the old lady
3 the grass in the Water Meadows
4 the river
5 the grass across the river
6 the cuckoo
7 Ben's attempts to see a wild animal
8 Ben's family
9 Ben's new house
10 the measles

My own work

A   Imagine that Ben continued to follow the little track he had found. Write a story about what happened next.

B   Now imagine that when he went home Ben wrote a letter to his friend in the town where he used to live, telling him about his new life in the country. Write Ben's letter.

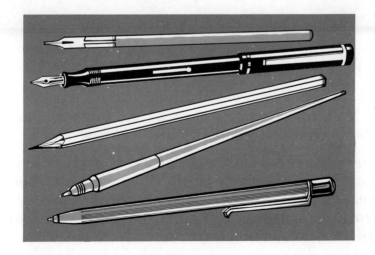

Perhaps the cottage in the picture is like the one Nosey Parker lived in.

1   Imagine the owner of the cottage in the picture decided to sell it. Make up an advertisement, headed **House for sale**, in which the owner described its five best features.

2   Now imagine someone looked round the house and was considering whether to buy it. This person found some faults as well as good features. Make two lists, one headed **Good features**, and the other **Faults**, that the person would consider before making a decision.

● Spelling

A   Near the end of the second paragraph of the passage is the word almost. Words beginning with <u>al</u> need careful spelling. Here are five more.

already   altogether   although   also   always

Write five sentences about Ben or Nosey Parker, including one of these words in each sentence.

B   Later in the passage you will find the words <u>rustle</u>, <u>weasel</u> and <u>measle</u>. Words ending in <u>el</u> and <u>le</u> also have to be spelt with care. Here are five more.

channel   middle   people   puddle   tunnel

Write five sentences about the countryside near Ben's house. In each sentence use one of the words listed above.

● Language

A   Look at the word <u>who</u> in the second sentence of the passage. In Unit 10 there was a question on joining sentences with the word <u>who</u>. Here are some more sentences to join in this way.

1   Ben could not play out with his brothers. They had measles.
2   Ben met Nosey Parker. She was coming out of her front door.
3   Nosey Parker was one of their neighbours. She was very old.
4   Later that day Ben went to bed early. He had a headache.
5   Next day the doctor came to see Ben. He had measles now.

B   The word <u>who</u> refers to **people**. The word <u>which</u> is used in the same way but refers to **things**. You will find the word <u>which</u> in the first two sentences of the last paragraph of the passage. Here are some sentences to join, using the word <u>which</u>.

1   Ben heard the call of the cuckoo. It changes its call in June.
2   He made tracks through the grass. It was thick and tall.
3   Ben had to take off his socks before he walked home. They were very wet.
4   He had expected to see some rabbits. Usually they were very active.
5   He knew the measle germs would attack him. They were like angry bees.

Hiding a horse in a hotel

One of the doors in the hotel corridor was open and Nicholas could hear a chambermaid humming to herself as she worked. He crept towards the door, hoping that he would be able to close it. And then he caught sight of a pile of blankets. He cautiously stretched out his hand and pulled a blanket towards him. It might come in handy. Suddenly he heard footsteps at the other end of the corridor. There was only one thing he could do. He unfolded the blanket and draped it over Danny so that not even his head was showing.

It was the porter. He stopped in front of Nicholas with a stern expression on his face.

"Where are you off to?" he said. Nicholas tried to sound nonchalant.

"I'm going to Room 119. We live there."

"And what's this then?" The porter pointed at the bundle of blanket that was Danny.

Nicholas swallowed. "This? Oh, this – well you see, it's Danny, my brother," he said. "We're playing horses. Gee up, Dan. Come along."

The porter looked at the disobedient bundle of blanket. "He doesn't seem to be very well trained yet. He won't do what you tell him," he said, laughing. "Off you go, up to your room; you mustn't carry on like this in the corridors. The hotel blankets aren't here for you to play with, you know."

Nicholas wanted to go at once, but Danny wouldn't budge. He just stood there under the blanket. "Come on, Danny, off we go." Nicholas felt desperate. All would be well if Danny kept quiet, but of course he didn't. He let out a funny neighing sound.

"Would you believe it," said the porter. "Quite a good imitation. Not bad at all. He ought to go on the stage, your brother." The porter was just about to pat Danny through the blanket, but fortunately at that moment Danny decided to move off, followed anxiously by Nicholas.

"Well I'm blessed, the things children get up to. You might almost think it was a real horse."

Nicholas led Danny past Auntie's door and into his own room. He turned the key twice in the lock.

"Quiet now, Danny, while I make you a stable in the cupboard," he said.

from 'A Pony in the Luggage' by Gunnel Linde

● Understanding

A   1   Why did Nicholas try to close the door in the corridor?
        2   Why do you think he turned the key **twice** in the lock in his own room?
        3   How do you know Danny was difficult to control?
        4   What was amusing about the porter's last remark?
        5   What was amusing about Nicholas's last remark?

B   Make a list of the moments when the porter nearly found out that the bundle in the blanket was a horse. In each case explain why he did **not** discover the truth.

● My own work

A   Imagine the passage was the middle part of a story about Nicholas and Danny, the horse.

Write the first part of the story, including why and how Nicholas got the horse into the hotel.

B   Write the last part of the story, describing what happened once Nicholas had got the horse into his room.

The hotel in the picture is probably like the one in which Nicholas was hiding Danny. Hotels often have many notices that give information or warnings to the guests. Design five eye-catching notices for a hotel. Each notice should deal with one of the following.

1 The name and address of the hotel
2 Information about meal times
3 A notice about lost property
4 A notice about dogs or pets
5 Information about fire precautions

Words

In the passage Nicholas was <u>desperate</u> when Danny would not move. He was <u>anxious</u> when he followed Danny down the corridor and he tried to be <u>nonchalant</u> (unconcerned) when the porter asked him where he was going.

The words underlined describe how Nicholas felt when certain things happened. Here are ten more adjectives about feelings.

happy	angry	worried	surprised	determined
ashamed	cautious	scared	puzzled	excited

Write a sentence about yourself for each one, choosing a suitable event to fit the word. The first one is begun for you.

1   I felt happy when ....

Language

A   Look at the sentence, near the middle of the passage, where the porter said, "You <u>mustn't</u> carry on like this in the corridors." The word <u>must</u> is usually used for strong rules and instructions.

Make a list of five more rules that might apply to behaviour in a hotel. Each rule should contain the word <u>must</u>.

B   The words <u>ought</u> and <u>should</u> are also used for rules and instructions but are not as strong as <u>must</u>. An example is "You <u>should</u> always leave a picnic site tidy."

Write five more sentences about the way people <u>should</u> or <u>ought to</u> behave in a park or the countryside.

Helping the kelpie

It seemed to Morag that the voice came from behind a big boulder at the edge of the burn. She got to her feet and looked round the other side of it, and there was a little old man as shrunken and shrivelled as a nut and all dripping wet.

"Well!" she said in amazement. "Who are you at all?"

"I am a kelpie, mistress," the little man snapped as cross as two sticks, and Morag began to laugh.

"Well," she said when she had done laughing, "so it's a kelpie that's in it! To think I should have lived to be seventy-two before I see a kelpie!" And she began to laugh again.

"Och, you have bad manners, old woman!" shouted the kelpie. "There is no need to laugh just because you see a kelpie!"

"Bad manners, is it!" Morag said sharply. "Then your manners will not mend mine if you talk so disrespectfully to your elders."

"You will be old before you are older than me," shouted he, "for I have lived in this burn for two hundred years!"

Morag was surprised at this, as well she might be, but she saw no reason to doubt what he said, and feeling sorry that she had offended him she said politely,

"Ah well, let us not quarrel over a hundred years or so. But I would like you to know that my name is Mistress Morag MacLeod."

"A good name," said the kelpie, polite in his turn. "And now, Mistress Morag, if you will look down here you will see that my foot is caught between two stones. I have not the strength to free it – not in the shape I am in at the moment, anyway."

He gave Morag a cunning look when he said this but she was looking at the place where his foot was caught and she did not see the expression on his face. She worked the stone away from his foot and the kelpie sat rubbing the ache the pressure of the stone had left in it.

"I am very grateful to you, Mistress Morag," he said. "I will give you some pearls from the big river to reward you."

from 'The Kelpie's Pearls' by Mollie Hunter

Understanding

A   Using clues from the passage explain how you know each of the following about the kelpie.

1   He was not really human.
2   He spent much of his life near water.
3   He was easily made angry.
4   He was sly.
5   He might be a danger to Morag.

B   Now write down five things you have learned about Morag.

My own work

A   The kelpie said he had been in the stream for two hundred years. Write a story about another meeting with a human being he had had during that time.

B   Imagine you were writing a folk-tale. Describe a creature (like the kelpie) you would include in your story.

We can see from the picture that the old man is a much pleasanter person than the kelpie. If we wanted to describe the old man **without** the picture we would have to include a lot of details about his appearance. Make a list of the details you would include in a description of the man in the picture.

Now do the same for someone you know well at your school.

Punctuation

The passage was mainly a conversation between Morag and the kelpie. In Unit 12 one of the questions reminded you to start a new paragraph each time the speaker changed during a conversation in a story.

Imagine you were able to ask the kelpie ten questions about himself. Write out the conversation you had. Begin your story, "One day I met the kelpie by the burn and started to ask him some questions."

Language

A   In the first paragraph of the passage are two words that are very similar in meaning: <u>shrunken</u> and <u>shrivelled</u>. Words that are similar in meaning are called **synonyms**.

Here are five words that are synonyms of words you can find in the first three paragraphs of the passage:

    large   rock   stream   astonishment   angry

Write down the five words from the passage that are synonyms of the words above.

B   Now here are five words from the last four paragraphs of the passage:

    quarrel   caught   cunning   expression   ache.

For each word write down a synonym.

The witch's broom

"You can take him," the old woman went on, and prodded the cat with her foot. "And don't say I never did you a good turn, my boy. Though, mind you, it's only half undone."

The Market Hall clock struck five as she spoke.

"It's getting awfully late," said Rosemary. "I think I must be going. Please may I have the broom?"

"The broom? Oh, aye, here you are." And so saying the old woman pushed it into Rosemary's hand, turned and disappeared down a dark alley at the side of the sweet shop. As she went under the arch she ducked her head as if she was used to a much taller kind of hat.

Rosemary watched her go. Then she looked down at the broom, and her heart sank. It was not what she wanted at all. It was the sort of broom that gardeners use – a rough wooden handle with a bundle of twigs bound on at one end, and only a few dilapidated twigs at that.

"What a shame!" said Rosemary. As the full extent of her bad luck dawned on her she could not stop the hot tears from trickling down her face. The broom was useless, at least for her purpose. She had no money left to buy another, and to crown it all she would have to walk all the way home without a buckle on her shoe, with not even the consolation of a toffee-apple. However, she was a brave little girl, and in the absence of a handkerchief she wiped her eyes with the back of her hand and decided to make the best of it. But just at that moment, quite clearly and distinctly, the cat said:

"It's a better bargain than it looks, you know."

"Who said that?" Rosemary could not believe her ears.

"Me, of course!" said the cat. "Oh, yes, of course I can talk. All animals can, but you can only hear me because you are holding the witch's broom."

Rosemary dropped it hurriedly. Then, realizing that she could not hear the cat talk without it, she picked it up again.

"And I should treat it with respect," went on the animal dryly. "There's not much life in the poor thing or she would not have sold it so cheap. Trust her for that!"

from 'Carbonel' by Barbara Sleigh

Understanding

A **1** What did you learn about Rosemary when she spoke for the first time?

     2 Why do you think she was so disappointed about the broom?

     3 Why do you think the author called her 'a brave little girl'?

     4 What made Rosemary change her mind about the broom?

     5 What else have you learned about Rosemary from the passage?

B   What did each of the following tell you about the old woman?

     1 the state of the broom
     2 the fact she had sold the broom to Rosemary
     3 the way she ducked her head under the arch
     4 her behaviour towards the cat
     5 the cat's attitude to her

My own work

A   Imagine you had the witch's broom for a day and could hear animals talking while you held it. Write a story about the day.

B   Imagine the broom had five other powers. What would you like these powers to be and why?

●   As the picture and passage suggest, witches have special clothes, equipment, spells, etc. Write down the names of ten things you would expect witches to have. Now make a **Witches' dictionary** from your list, putting the words in alphabetical order and writing for each one a suitable **definition** or meaning.

100

Words

A   In the passage there is a short but clear description of a gardener's broom: '. . . a rough wooden handle with a bundle of twigs bound on at one end.'

Write similar descriptions of these five objects found in a garden:

spade   flower-pot   rake   wheelbarrow   greenhouse

B   Imagine the author had also described these objects that are mentioned in the passage.

alley   arch   buckle   toffee-apple   handkerchief

Write out the descriptions the author would have written.

Language

A   In Units 2 and 14 there were questions on using an **apostrophe** when a letter is missed out in a word. There are five examples of this use of the apostrophe in the passage. Write down the five sentences in which the words occur and underline the words that use an apostrophe in this way.

B   Now look at these two parts of sentences from the passage:
'The old woman pushed it into Rosemary's hand.'
'You can only hear me because you are holding the witch's broom.'

In these two sentences the apostrophe is used in order to show **possession**, not because a letter has been missed out.

Write out each of the following sentences and underline the words that have apostrophes to show possession.

1   Rosemary met the old woman when she was doing her mother's shopping.
2   She was surprised when she saw the old woman's broom.
3   The cat's life with the witch had not been very happy.
4   Rosemary decided to take the cat to her grandmother's house.
5   It had been a very odd day in the girl's life.

The bird that disappeared

"Hallo, what are *you* up to?"

Hattie glowered at Rudolf, who sat over the fridge as if nothing at all had happened.

"Getting your food," she said; at which he repeated his one remark, and made Hattie think he was rather a stupid bird. She knew he couldn't help it, but she would much rather have been left to look after a little dog. She sighed and went to get Rudolf's seed. He seemed to have spilt all his water, too, so she had to open both sides of the cage in order to get out the two plastic containers. They really needed cleaning; she thought Aunt Fred would be pleased with her if she did that as well. She scrubbed them thoroughly with Vim, and gazed at the rainbow colours the sunlight made on the bubbles in the water. The sun was beginning to go down across the field; it must be well past tea-time. Hattie made a very good resolution to finish Rudolf and then get Aunt Fred some really nice tea on a tray, with thin bread-and-butter. She went to the cage to put back the clean white containers.

Rudolf had gone.

Hattie stood up on a stool to see if he was hiding somewhere in a corner at the bottom of his cage; but he wasn't. She realized with horror that the places where the containers fitted left holes . . . And not only that, but Tony had left the back door wide open, too.

Hattie called, whistled, rushed round looking behind the fridge, under the table, in the china cupboard, along the tops of the curtains, in all the saucepans on the shelf. No Rudolf. She came to the terrible conclusion that he must have got out of the back door.

She went outside. There was the fatal bird-bath, now right way up; but no birds anywhere near it, let alone Rudolf. She dashed round the garden, making what she imagined might be Rudolf-noises: chirps, squeaks, more whistles. Not a sign. She remembered being told that if budgies escaped, other wild birds killed them: and Rudolf, with his chewed tail, would stand even less chance than a whole-tailed budgie. She knew that Aunt Fred would be horribly upset to lose him: and she was already upset enough about being in bed, with two cracked feet.

from 'The Smoke in Albert's Garden' by Jenifer Wayne

Understanding

1 Why do you think Hattie was looking after Rudolf?
2 What was the one remark that Rudolf could make?
3 What made Hattie think Rudolf was a stupid bird?
4 Why did Hattie decide to clean the containers?
5 Why did she take so long to clean them?
6 What was the mistake that Hattie made?
7 What other mistake had been made?
8 How did Hattie try to make up for the mistakes?
9 What did she fear had happened to Rudolf?
10 What do you think upset Hattie most of all?

My own work

A   The passage gives hints that some rather strange things had happened earlier. Aunt Fred now had two cracked feet and Rudolf a chewed tail.

Write a story that describes how these things happened.

B   Sometimes when a budgie escapes its owners advertise in the local newspaper for help in trying to find it. Make up a suitable advertisement, describing Rudolf, for the newspaper.

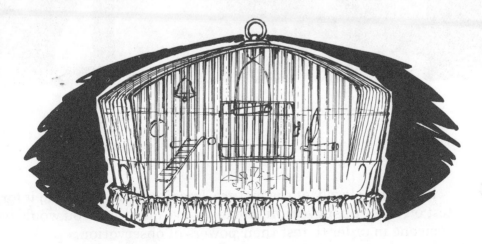

Look very closely at the picture. Imagine you were using it for a test on **close observation**. Make up five questions you would ask someone in order to test their powers of observation.

Words

A   In Unit 23 there was a question about **synonyms** (words similar in meaning). Look at the word <u>glowered</u> in the second line of the passage. It seems the right word to choose from many other words that are synonyms of <u>looked</u>.

Here are five more synonyms of <u>looked</u>. Use each word in a sentence about Hattie and Rudolf.

    glanced   stared   inspected   peeped   watched

B   Here are five words from the last paragraph of the passage. Write down a good synonym for each.

    went   dashed   imagined   remembered   upset

Language

A   Find words in the passage that have these **endings**.

1 _____ ed (a verb in the past tense)
2 _____ tion (a noun)
3 _____ ible (an adjective)
4 _____ ly (an adverb)
5 _____ sion (a noun)

B   All the words you found in Part A had endings which were added to another word (or part of another word). These endings are called **suffixes**.

Here are five more suffixes. For each one write down two words you know, ending with that suffix.

    _____ ing
    _____ ment
    _____ ness
    _____ ful
    _____ est

In the empty castle

For a while Joseph was content to lean on the battlements and look out over the strange view. Now and then bumble-bees flew past droning like helicopters. Once a butterfly paused beside him on the castle roof, flaunting wings of scarlet and black that were as big as sails. Like sails they flapped lazily, wafting a smell of flower pollen, then were pressed tightly together upright and showed a quite different marble design underneath. Joseph stroked them and found that they felt like feathers. Finally the butterfly flew off, lurching to left and to right wildly like a kite, but seeming to know where it was going.

The afternoon seemed long all alone in the empty castle. Joseph explored it again, looking out of all the windows. This time he found another bedroom just under the roof. It had the same rolled fern curtains and a beautiful round nest made entirely of new moss, exactly the right size for him. It had a coverlet of woven cobweb and thistledown. At one side of the nest was a leaf of lamb's tongue, furry side up for a bedside mat.

Joseph wanted to put something of his own in the room to show it was his. Things of one's own are home-making. He felt in all his pockets. Matches – but he wanted to keep those with him. String, a pebble, a shell, a pencil-sharpener, a birthday card with a picture of a jet airliner, a crumpled piece of gold chocolate paper that had covered a whole layer of chocolates. But as he feared, his other real treasure had rolled out.

He put the pebble and the shell on his windowsill as ornaments. Then he hung the picture of the jet on a convenient twig and sat down to look round him with pleasure. Certainly it was now his room. He put the string back in his pocket and picked up the pencil-sharpener. It gave him an idea, and he went and fetched a piece of broken nut out of the sack. He pressed it into the pencil-sharpener and turned. Out of the top came delicate curly slices of nut, crisp like super cornflakes.

from 'The Castle of Yew' by Lucy Boston

Understanding

A   The title of a story should be short but give a good idea of what the story is about. This passage already has a title. Choose a title of your own.

Now choose a title for each of the four paragraphs.

B   What did Joseph find interesting about each of the following?

1   the bumble-bees
2   the wings of the butterfly
3   the bedroom
4   the things he found in his pockets
5   the pieces of broken nut

My own work

A   Joseph found all kinds of things when he emptied his pockets. Empty your pockets or anything else in which you keep things. Put the things on a table, describe them and say where they came from.

B   The castle bedroom is described in the second paragraph of the passage. Write a description of **your** bedroom.

Castles, like those in the picture and passage, are buildings where great rulers lived. Use an encyclopaedia to find out information about each of the castles listed below. All of them can still be visited today. Write down the name of each castle and write a few notes about each one to show why it is famous. Give your work a suitable heading.

Tower of London   Windsor Castle   Edinburgh Castle

Caernarvon Castle   Maiden Castle

Words

There are a number of difficult words in the passage. Write down the meaning of each of the following. If you are not sure, try to work out the meaning from the sense of the sentence.

content	lurching
droning	crumpled
flaunting	convenient
flapped	delicate
wafting	crisp

Now check your answers in a dictionary.

Language

A   Commas are used to separate the items in a list. Write out the sentence in the third paragraph of the passage where commas are used in this way.

B   Sometimes a comma is needed in a sentence for other reasons, for example to show a pause.

Commas are used in the last sentence of each of the four paragraphs of the passage. Write out the four sentences **without** putting in the commas.

Now put in the commas where the author put them and explain why you think they were needed.

The Sea

The sea is a hungry dog,
Giant and grey.
He rolls on the beach all day.
With his clashing teeth and shaggy jaws
Hour upon hour he gnaws
The rumbling, tumbling stones,
And 'Bones, bones, bones, bones!'
The giant sea-dog moans,
Licking his greasy paws.

And when the night wind roars
And the moon rocks in the stormy cloud,
He bounds to his feet and snuffs and sniffs,
Shaking his wet sides over the cliffs,
And howls and hollos long and loud.

But on quiet days in May or June,
When even the grasses on the dune
Play no more their reedy tune,
With his head between his paws
He lies on the sandy shores,
So quiet, so quiet, he scarcely snores.

James Reeves

Understanding

A   Each of the three verses describes the sea at a different time. What time does each verse describe and how is the sea different?

B   In the poem the sea is compared to a dog. Make a list of ten words and phrases that seem to you to help to make a good comparison between the sea and a dog.

My own work

A   The second verse of the poem describes a stormy night. Describe a storm you remember, saying what it was like, what you felt and what damage it did.

B   Sometimes large ships are wrecked at sea in stormy weather. Imagine you were a passenger on a ship that was wrecked in a storm. Write a story about your adventures.

The picture of a waterfall and a pool, and the poem about the sea and waves make you think of the many names that are used for types of water. Make a word-list of ten words that name different types of water. Begin your list with <u>waterfall</u>, <u>pool</u>, <u>waves</u>. Give your list a suitable title.

Words

A   Pairs of words beginning with the same sound are often used in poetry. A good example in the poem is <u>snuffs</u> and <u>sniffs</u> in the second verse. These words suggest a dog very well.

What do you think would fit each of the following pairs of words?

1   slimy and slippery   4   wild and wicked
2   cruel and crafty   5   rough and rugged
3   soft and soothing

B   Think of two words, beginning with the same sound, that would describe each of the following.

1   sand   4   a stone wall
2   ice   5   a thick blanket
3   fallen leaves

Language

A   In Units 23 and 25 there were questions about **synonyms**. Choose suitable synonyms for these **verbs** from the poem.

   gnaws   moans   roars   bounds   lies

B   Synonyms are words similar in meaning. Words opposite in meaning are called **antonyms**. If you look at the last two verses of the poem you could say that one describes the <u>noisy</u> sounds of the storm and the other the <u>quiet</u> days of summer. <u>Noisy</u> and <u>quiet</u> are antonyms.

Complete these sentences by including pairs of words that are antonyms of each other.

1   In a storm the sea seems _____ but when there is no wind it is _____.
2   Sand is _____ to touch but rocks are _____.
3   In August the beach is often _____ but in winter it is _____.
4   When the sun shines all the holidaymakers are _____, but if it rains they may be _____.
5   Some people like to go on a _____ holiday but others want a _____ holiday.

unit 28

The island

Carey's first thought was that she wished she had brought her hat. The white sand flung back the dazzling glare of the sunlight in such a way that she had to screw up her eyes to see.

The bed had done its best for them. It had set them down on the very tip of a horse-shoe shaped reef. They found themselves on a thin strip of fine white sand held in place by walls of pitted coral. It was almost like being on a ship. In the distance, across a lagoon of dazzling blue sea, they could see the other tip of the horse-shoe. In between, a mile or so away, where the front of the horse-shoe might be, were trees and low hills.

In among the rocks, which formed the coral walls of their narrow strip of land, were clear pools in which glimmered seaweed of lovely colours, sea anemones, and transparent fish. And the sand was as smooth and fine and white as icing sugar. They had never seen sand like it. There were four great scrapes in it where the bed had come to rest, but beyond that not a footmark, not a ripple.

Charles kicked off his bedroom slippers and let his bare feet sink into the warm crust. It spurted up between his toes. "Gosh," he said happily.

Carey peered over at the lagoon. It was deep and clear. They could see strange fish swimming through the sunlit water. "How lovely!" exclaimed Carey. "How wonderful! Do let's go and explore." Out at sea, between the two points of the horse-shoe, great waves rolled up and broke into swirls of spray, spreading their foam into the smooth surface of the lagoon.

Miss Price was unpacking. She took four bottles of ginger-pop out of the string bag and placed them in a pool to keep cool. The rest of the food, the hard-boiled eggs and the sandwiches, she put under the bed in the shade.

"You two big ones can explore," she announced, "but I'm going to sit here in the sun." She retrieved her umbrella, her book and the broomstick. Then sitting down on the sand, with her back against the bed, she methodically removed her shoes and stockings. Miss Price's feet, Carey noticed, were as pink and knobbly as her hands.

from 'Bedknob and Broomstick' by Mary Norton

114

Understanding

A   What have you learned about each of the following?

    1 Charles
    2 Carey
    3 Miss Price
    4 the bed
    5 the journey to the island

B   Answer these questions about the island. Give a reason for each answer.

    1 What sort of climate did the island have?
    2 What sort of beach did the island have?
    3 What was the sea like round the island?
    4 What was the interior of the island like?
    5 In what part of the world was the island?

My own work

A   Imagine you have discovered a beautiful island (like the one described in the passage). Draw a careful, detailed map of it and then describe it in words, as if for the opening page of a story.

B   Now describe an adventure that took place on your island.

As well as tropical islands like those in the picture and the passage there are many other islands all over the world. Here are the names of ten well-known islands.

Crete	Cyprus	Easter Island	Iceland	Jamaica
Jersey	Mauritius	Newfoundland	Sicily	Tasmania

Copy out the list of islands and find each one on a map of the world in an atlas. Use the index or **gazetteer** at the back of the atlas to help you find the islands. When you have found each island tick it on your list.

Spelling

A   A number of words in the passage have a **double consonant**, for example <u>dazzling</u> and <u>ripple</u>. Make a list of five more words in the passage that have double consonants.

B   Look at the words <u>sitting</u> and <u>biting</u>.

<u>Sitting</u> has a double <u>t</u> because the <u>i</u> sound before the <u>t</u> is **short**. <u>Biting</u> has only one <u>t</u> because the <u>i</u> sound before the <u>t</u> is **long**.

Always look at the **vowel** sound when you are deciding whether or not the word needs a double consonant.

Here are five pairs of words. In each case choose the word that is correctly spelt and use it in a sentence about the island.

1	stoped	stopped	**4** hiden	hidden
2	runing	running	**5** begining	beginning
3	shining	shinning		

Language

A   In Unit 18 there was an exercise on making interesting **comparisons**. In the passage find the sentence where the sand was compared to icing sugar. This type of comparison, where one thing is compared to another, is called a **simile**.

Here are five similes to complete.

1   The sea was as smooth as ....
2   The coral was as sharp as ....
3   Charles' feet felt as warm as ....
4   Carey was as happy as ....
5   Miss Price's knees were as knobbly as ....

B   Good similes make your writing interesting. Imagine you were writing a story about a day in your life. Complete each of the following with an interesting simile.

1   My toothpaste tasted like ....
2   The burnt toast smelled like ....
3   At the start of the day the classroom looked like ....
4   When I sharpened my pencil, the point felt like ....
5   At play-time the noise sounded like ....

The crane driver saves the circus

One day the crane driver had to unload a circus train. It was a very hot day. By noontime, the iron girders were hot enough to burn one's fingers. By three o'clock in the afternoon, it was as hot as the Sahara. The lions and tigers and all the other animals thought of the jungle or the desert and grew restless. They raged and roared and hurled themselves with all their might against the doors of their cages, loosening the locks. Their howling and roaring sounded like hell on earth. Their keepers trembled and hid in empty tar barrels. Finally, trumpeting, snorting, and thundering were heard – as if the devil himself had broken loose. The keepers cried out in desperation, "Holy St Castulus, save us!" They crouched even lower in their barrels, thinking their last hour had come. And then, charging across the loading site, came not the devil himself, but the elephant. That was just as bad, however, because by now he had sunstroke. He knocked over the trucks, trampled the engines, and hurled crates, cows, and pigs into the air as if they were toys. Lektro's brother, the man who drove the ox team, drove his team away as quickly as he could, for the oxen belonged to him.

A lady circus rider called, "Come on, Jumbo, calm down, and we'll give you a bunch of bananas!"

But the elephant paid no attention. He got wilder and wilder until Lektro finally shouted, "Better get a gun!"

The director of the circus shouted even louder, "Don't shoot! Don't shoot! That elephant cost five thousand pounds!" By now, the locks on the doors of the lions' cages had worked very loose indeed.

The crane driver was watching all this from the top of his crane. He was worried. He thought, "They're in real trouble down there". He clutched the lever with both hands and prayed, "Dear God, please let him come a little closer to the crane so I can catch him with the grab." And as the elephant charged, quick as lightning the crane driver dropped the grab over him. The elephant lashed out wildly with legs, ears, and trunk as he was lifted into the air. The girders strained. But the iron held firm; there had been no flaw in its casting. The crane driver dangled the raging elephant over the river, dipping him in and out of the water until he had been cured of sunstroke.

from 'The Crane' by Reiner Zimnik

Understanding

A   The circus was in great danger. How did the behaviour of each of the following make the danger seem more and more serious?

1   the lions and tigers
2   the keepers
3   the elephant
4   Lektro's brother
5   Lektro

B   In Unit 5 there was an exercise on using short sentences to make a story more exciting.

There are good examples in the passage. Write down each of the following sentences and explain why each of them adds excitement at that point of the story.

1   It was a very hot day.
2   But the elephant paid no attention.
3   He was worried.
4   The girders strained.

Now write a short sentence of your own to start the next paragraph of the passage. This sentence should show that there was still danger to the circus.

My own work

Imagine that the animals soon calmed down, the circus was unloaded and the first performance was held the next day.

Write a story about your visit to the circus that day. Don't forget to include in the story how you felt before you went as well as the actual performance.

The picture shows a large building as it is being built. A crane is being used, probably much bigger than the one described in the passage.

Before a building is built, accurate plans have to be made, carefully drawn to scale and labelled. Make an accurate plan of your school and label the rooms and other parts of the building.

Spelling

A   All the following words occur in the passage:

enough   broken   cried   across   knocked
quickly   paid   loose   dropped   until

   They are all words that are often mis-spelt. Write out the words in alphabetical order, making sure you know how each is spelt.

B   Now use each of the words in a sentence about things you own or things you have done.

Language revision

1   From the first paragraph of the passage write down five **verbs** that are in the **past tense**.
2   Look at the words spoken by the lady circus rider. Which verb is in the **future tense**?
3   Which word in the last sentence of the first paragraph is a **collective noun**?
4   Write down the **adjective** that is in the last part of the fourth sentence of the passage. What is the **comparative** of this adjective?
5   Write down the **simile** in the fourth sentence. Find another simile in the last paragraph.
6   Use the word who to form one sentence from the first two sentences of the last paragraph.
7   Near the end of the passage is a sentence that describes the elephant as it lashed out. What is the **adverb** in this sentence?
8   The same sentence contains **commas**. Why are commas used in this sentence? In what different way is a comma used in the last sentence of the passage?
9   Look at the words spoken by the director of the circus. Why do you think the author used the word that and not this?
10 Write a sentence of your own that sums up the events of the passage.

Finding things to do

All the Melendy children had their own jobs. They each had not one but several. For instance, they made their own beds and took weekly turns at cleaning the Office (all except Oliver, of course). And the cleaning had to be thorough. Under Cuffy's eagle eye there could be no nonsense such as sweeping things under things, or shaking the mop out of the window, or dusting only where it showed. It had to be well done. In addition to these there were the special jobs. Rush shined all the shoes, took care of the fuse-box, repaired the radio when necessary, and was sort of plumber's assistant to Willy Sloper. Mona helped Cuffy with the mending and ironing, and had the entire responsibility of keeping the living-room tidy. Randy always set the dinner table and dried the dishes, as well as sorting the laundry and making out the lists. Even Oliver had his chores. He had to water all the plants, and feed the fish and his turtle, and see that the clay in the tub was kept moist.

So between jobs and school and amusing themselves life for the Melendys rarely contained a dull moment.

This, however, was one of them.

"I'm so b-o-o-o-o-red!" groaned Randy, lifting one foot in the air and letting it drop heavily as though simply unable to sustain the weight of her boredom.

"You and me, both," agreed Rush.

"And I'm bored listening to you complain," complained Mona, slapping her book together.

Oliver paid no attention to any of them. "Why don't we play something? Parcheesi or something?" suggested Mona.

"Oh par*cheesi*!" scoffed Randy.

"Well, you used to like it. Then how about making something out of clay, or drawing, or we might do a play."

"Clay's dreary on a wet day, and I'm tired of drawing, and it's no fun being in plays with you, Mona, because you take all the leading parts, and Rush and I are only the fathers and mothers or the maids or the policemen or something."

"Oh, all right, you're impossible!" Mona retired to her book. "Why don't you read?"

"I've read everything," said Randy, which wasn't true, but she was enjoying being difficult. It was a novelty.

from 'The Saturdays' by Elizabeth Enright

Understanding

A 1 Six people were mentioned in the passage. Which of the six do you think were the Melendy children?

2 Why do you think Oliver did not have to clean the Office?

3 The last paragraph said that Randy was 'being difficult'. How was she being difficult?

4 What was Mona doing when she was not arguing with Randy?

5 What do you think Rush was doing?

B Find each of the following phrases in the passage. What do you think each of them means?

1 took weekly turns
2 Cuffy's eagle eye
3 Oliver had his chores
4 the leading parts
5 It was a novelty.

My own work

A The children mentioned some of the things they played or did when they were not at school or looking after the house.

Describe some of the games you play in the house or outside.

B Choose one game you particularly like and imagine you have met someone who has never played it. Explain the game and the rules clearly.

In 'My own work' you were asked to describe some of the games you play. Here is a chance to write a book about games.

Choose three ball games and write a chapter about each one. Use an encyclopaedia to help you find information about the history of the game. Include in your chapter how the game is played, why you enjoy playing it and any other information you think is suitable.

For your book you will need a title page, a contents page and a short introduction in which you explain what your book is about. Include drawings and diagrams where you think they are suitable and make an attractive cover for your book.

Sentences

A   The first paragraph of the passage listed the jobs that the children did in the house. Choose a job that **all** the children had to do and write a sentence explaining what the job was.

Now write a sentence for each of the children, in each case describing **one** job the child had to do.

B   Write five sentences about jobs **you** do at home or at school.

Language revision

1   Look at the fifth sentence of the passage. Write down the words ending in <u>ing</u> and the **verbs** from which they are formed.

2   Make up a rule that the children had to obey in the house. Include in the rule the best word from <u>ought</u>, <u>should</u>, <u>must</u>.

3   Look at these two phrases from the passage:
   'Under Cuffy's eagle eye ....'
   'Clay's dreary on a wet day ....'
   In each case explain why an **apostrophe** is used.

4   The **phrase** "Under Cuffy's eagle eye" is a good way to begin a sentence. Why?

5   Look at the sentence where Randy said she was bored. Which word has a **prefix** that changes the meaning of the word?
   Look at the last word of the same sentence. Write down another word that has the same **suffix**.

6   Look at the words <u>weight</u> and <u>air</u> in the same sentence. These words sound the same as two other words but have different meanings. Write down the two other words.

7   Write down the three different **conjunctions** that are used in the third paragraph from the end of the passage.

8   In the first part of the same paragraph two words can be found that are **antonyms** of each other. What are the two words? Now find a **synonym** for each of these words in the second paragraph of the passage.

9   During the children's conversation which rule is followed about paragraphs?

10 Write a sentence of your own about the argument between Mona and Randy.

Book list

Prudence Andrew	Mr. Morgan's Marrow (Hamish Hamilton)
Elisabeth Beresford	The Secret Railway (Methuen Children's Books)
Lucy Boston	The Castle of Yew (Bodley Head)
Richard Carpenter	Catweazle (Penguin)
Beverly Cleary	Ramona the Pest (Hamish Hamilton)
Meindert De Jong	Shadrach (Lutterworth Press)
Edward Eager	The Time Garden (Macmillan)
Elizabeth Enright	The Saturdays (Heinemann)
Rosemary Garland	The Canary Shop (Hamish Hamilton)
Griselda Gifford	Ben's Expedition (Bodley Head)
Jacynth Hope-Simpson	The Edge of the World (Hamish Hamilton)
Mollie Hunter	The Kelpie's Pearls (Blackie)
Norman Hunter	The Home-made Dragon (Bodley Head)
Clive King	Stig of the Dump (Penguin)
Gunnel Linde	A Pony in the Luggage (Dent)
Astrid Lindgren	Pippi Longstocking (Oxford University Press)
Margaret Mahy	The Bus Under the Leaves (Dent)
Rosemary Manning	Green Smoke (Longman Young Books)
Mary Norton	Bedknob and Broomstick (Dent)
P. D. Pemberton	Richard's M-Class Cows (Faber)
Barbara Sleigh	Carbonel (Macdonald & Janes)
Edith Unnerstad	Little O (Michael Joseph)
Jenifer Wayne	The Smoke in Albert's Garden (Heinemann)
Barbara Willard	The Reindeer Slippers (Hamish Hamilton)
Reiner Zimnik	The Crane (Hodder & Stoughton Children's Books)

Acknowledgements

Thanks are due to the following publishers, agents and authors for permission to reprint the copyright material indicated. Every effort has been made to trace the ownership of all copyright material, but in a few cases this has proved impossible. Should any question arise as to the use of any extract, or any error, it is hoped that the publishers will be informed.

Hamish Hamilton Ltd. for extracts from *Ramona the Pest* by Beverly Cleary, *Mr. Morgan's Marrow* by Prudence Andrew, *The Canary Shop* by Rosemary Garland, and *The Edge of the World* by Jacynth Hope-Simpson; Dorothy Brown Thompson for the poem *Getting Back* from *An Invitation to Poetry* published by Addison-Wesley Publishing Company; Laurence Pollinger Ltd. for an extract from *Shadrach* by Meindert De Jong, published by the Lutterworth Press; Edith Unnerstad for an extract from *Little O*, published by Michael Joseph Ltd; J. M. Dent & Sons Ltd. for extracts from *The Bus Under the Leaves* by Margaret Mahy, *A Pony in the Luggage* by Gunnel Linde, and *Bedknob and Broomstick* by Mary Norton; David Higham Associates Ltd. for an extract from *The Reindeer Slippers* by Barbara Willard, published by Hamish Hamilton Ltd; The Bodley Head for extracts from *The Home-made Dragon* by Norman Hunter, *Ben's Expedition* by Griselda Gifford, and *The Castle of Yew* by Lucy Boston, all published by the Bodley Head; Oxford University Press for an extract from *Pippi Longstocking* by Astrid Lindgren, translated by Edna Hurup (1954); Penguin Books Ltd. for an extract from *Green Smoke* (Longman Young Books, 1957) pp.15–16 © 1957 by Rosemary Manning; Shufunotomo Co., Ltd. for the poem *Hurry Home* by Leonard Clark, from *Here and There*, published by The Hamlyn Group; Faber and Faber Ltd. for an extract from *Richard's M-Class Cows* by P. D. Pemberton; Macmillan, London and Basingstoke, for an extract from *The Time Garden* by Edward Eager; Methuen Children's Books Ltd. for an extract from *The Secret Railway* by Elisabeth Beresford; Murray Pollinger for an extract from *Stig of the Dump* by Clive King, published by Penguin Books Ltd; Bernard Gillman Ltd. for an extract from *Catweazle* by Richard Carpenter, published by Penguin Books Ltd; A. M. Heath & Co. Ltd. for an extract from *The Kelpie's Pearls* by Mollie Hunter, published by Blackie and Son Ltd; Harvey Unna & Stephen Durbridge Ltd. for an extract from *Carbonel* by Barbara Sleigh, published by Macdonald & Janes Publishers Ltd; William Heinemann Ltd. for extracts from *The Smoke in Albert's Garden* by Jenifer Wayne, *The Saturdays* by Elizabeth Enright, and the poem *The Sea* from *The Wandering Moon* by James Reeves; Hodder & Stoughton Children's Books for an extract from *The Crane* by Reiner Zimnik.